THE PLEROMIC LIGHT UNVEILED

The
Pleromic Light
Unveiled:

An Instructive Monograph on the
HOLY GNOSTIC LITURGY
OF THE PLEROMIC LIGHT

by Tau Phosphoros

Archbishop and Patriarch of the
APOSTOLIC CHURCH OF THE PLEROMA

TriadPress
Hainesville, IL

The Pleromic Light Unveiled: An Instructive Monograph on the Holy Gnostic Liturgy of the Pleromic Light

Published August 2018

ISBN: 978-1-946814-06-7

Triad Press, LLC
260 E. Belvidere Rd. #357
Hanesville, IL 60030

http://pleromachurch.org

To the Holiest St. Martha,
who has guided me, protected me,
taken care of me, and purified my soul,
this work is reverently dedicated.

Table of Contents

Introduction

A study of the Holy Gnostic Liturgy of the Pleromic Light must begin with at least a short discussion of its origin and development. This Mass began, in fact, not as a liturgy for the Apostolic Church of the Pleroma, nor even for the Ecclesia Gnostica Catholica Hermetica (of which the ACP is the direct spiritual heir), but within the Parish of St. Michael the Archangel of the Eglise Gnostique Catholique Apostolique, under the late regionary bishop, the Most Rev. Robert Cokinis, from whom I received my Minor Order ordinations. It was indeed upon his comment made to me one evening, sitting in his kitchen in Bellwood, Illinois, that he wished to see more "Gnostic elements" in the Mass, that I was inspired to begin work upon a new liturgy. The first draft of this liturgy appeared in December 2000, as "The Hermetic Vespers." This abbreviated liturgy was intended for use with pre-consecrated elements, not containing any rite of transubstantiation. Within a few months, the "Hermetic Vespers" evolved into the Holy Gnostic Liturgy of the Hermetic Rose+Croix, which quickly became the preferred liturgical rite of St. Michael's Parish, because of its powerful theurgical effects that were recognized by all who experienced it.

Although incredibly popular with the clergy and ever-growing congregation of St. Michael's, and although the elements of the Hermetic Rose+Croix liturgy fell firmly within established tradition, there were some among +Cokinis' clergy and confreres who accused St. Michael's of being "innovators" which, apparently, was intended to suggest that we were not honoring tradition. The misunderstanding of +Cokinis with regard to what was performed and accomplished at St. Michael's was compounded because of our close relationship with certain bishops within the episcopal lineage of the Most Rev. Michael-Paul Bertiaux. This led to an ultimatum being issued by bishop Cokinis to the entire Parish of St. Michael the Archangel to either cease

1

the practice of the Hermetic Liturgy and to cut all ties with bishops William Behun and Martin Jacobs, or face excommunication. The clergy of St. Michael's, with the consent of its congregants, chose to continue its efficacious work and to maintain its relationship with bishops Behun and Jacobs, who proved to be true friends and allies of St. Michael's. The lone Parish of St. Michael the Archangel continued to operate with the Very Rev. Fr. Kenneth Canterbury as Priest-in-charge (and Br. Anthony Angelo and myself as Acolytes) as the Ecclesia Gnostica Catholica Hermetica. I would receive the Diaconate and Priesthood over the course of the year 2001 at the hands of +William Behun; and, after having issued a Bull of Election in March 2002, the Most Rev. William Behun, assisted by the late bishop Martin Jacobs, elevated to the sacred order of the episcopate Frs. Kenneth Canterbury, Anthony Angelo, and myself on Saturday, April 27, 2002, at Kenosha, Wisconsin, at a High Mass of the Holy and Apostolic Church of the Third Age.

It is not my intention here to delve too deeply into ecclesiastical history, as this has already been documented in great detail within the private discourses of the ACP. But some context is necessary to explain how our present liturgy has come to be. In any case, on April 28, 2002, exactly one year to the day from the inaugural celebration of the Liturgy of the Hermetic Rose+Croix, a Parish Charter was drawn up for St. Michael the Archangel by the new Sovereign Triad of the EGCH (Tau Cephas, Tau Mercurius, and myself, Tau Valentinus), and delivered to myself. Over the next couple of years, bishop Canterbury and I expanded the Hermetic Rose+Croix liturgy into the Holy Gnostic Liturgy of the Hermetic Light. The Sovereign Triad would be disbanded in early 2007 in order to invest full Patriarchal authority in the Most Rev. Kenneth Canterbury; but bishop Canterbury would dissolve the EGCH entirely before the end of 2008. While seemingly unfortunate at the time, the Spirit of the Church was already stirring to manifest itself in a new vehicle. This powerful egregore, largely ignored and neglected by the other two-thirds of the former Sovereign Triad, revealed its will to me to manifest; to be re-born into a new body suitable to its nature. The Liturgy of the Hermetic Light was modified very slightly to become the present Liturgy of the Pleromic Light, the principal liturgy of the Apostolic Church of the Pleroma, which was instituted at the Feast of Holy Pentecost, May 31, 2009. To be sure, the ACP is *not* the EGCH, any more than the reincarnated soul is its previous persona. But the Spirit that animated the former is truly that which animates the latter. And this is verified through continual revelation and through the efficacy of our work.

The Liturgy of the Pleromic Light, the central rite of the ACP, is nothing less than an operation of High Theurgy; it is, in fact, the very highest of theurgical rites. As a Church of the Holy Gnosis, there are a number of theurgical practices that our clergy undertake on a regular basis, from those published in the *ACP Clergy Handbook* – which are, in fact, among the most effective, being based upon the structure of the Mass – to those issued privately through the Christian Knights of Saint-Martin and other affiliated bodies of the Church. All of these operations have very specific and important roles to play in the repertoire of spiritual tools which may be called upon as a means of aid to our fellow souls in need of physical, mental, and spiritual assistance, and of spiritual and psychical warfare against the dark and malign forces that threaten the well-being and peaceful evolution of humanity. The Holy Eucharist, though, is that one that is absolutely indispensable. That is not to say that it may replace any of the other Works; but it unquestionably takes precedence over all others, as it gives us an unparalleled spiritual sustenance. It may be likened to the maintenance of the physical body. We must eat and drink in order to survive. This does not negate the need to bathe, brush our teeth, get adequate exercise, etc., etc. However, it does not matter how clean you are if you do not have sufficient nourishment to

3

maintain all of the body's functions. And that is precisely the relationship of the Mass to all other spiritual and theurgical practices. One might not spiritually "die" without the Mass, since some amount of sustenance can be obtained through prayer, etc., but for the theurgist, the true spiritual warrior, the Mass provides the "strong meat" necessary to sustain his or her ongoing efforts towards the regeneration of humanity.

Every part of the Mass is important, nothing is extraneous. From the layout of the Temple, to the items and vestments utilized; as well as every word spoken and every gesture made, from the Preliminary Rites to the Dismissal. Now, it is not my intention to offer a *comprehensive* analysis here, as this is merely a booklet and not a full treatment, although I would not rule out such an endeavor at some future time. But even were this a large volume devoted to the subject, the mysteries of the Mass are as inexhaustible as its spiritual benediction. But I think that it will be of great benefit to many to give a brief but detailed analysis of each part of the Eucharistic service. This was done in part in our paper on "The Alchemy of the Eucharist" which appears in the *Clergy Handbook*, and to which I shall make reference in the present work, but that survey really only addresses the specifically *alchemical* aspects of the liturgy; and while I am generally of the mind that the alchemical process suitably explains the entire technical process of the Mass, there is certainly much else to be explored therein. Before proceeding therewith, let us briefly examine the general layout of this short treatise. The organization of this monograph is not into chapters as ordinarily formed. Rather, there are three primary sections corresponding to the three principal phases of alchemy: Black, White, and Red. The further sub-divisions simply follow the natural divisions of the Mass.

The Black Phase

In the alchemical parlance, the Black Phase refers to the initial preparatory operations. The two principal operations in this phase are the *Calcination* and the *Dissolution*. Let us quote briefly from the "Alchemy of the Eucharist" (*ACP Clergy Handbook*, pp. 323-324):

The Calcination begins in the antechamber, during the period of preparation, and silent meditation and reflection. It continues throughout the opening invocations and purification rituals such as the Asperges and the Censing of the Altar; culminating in the Confiteor and Absolution, wherein the celebrants and participants are made pure by the power of Christ, thus preventing contamination of the Eucharistic Operation; and concluding with the Sign of Peace.

Dissolution begins with the First Hermetic Discourse. The substance extracted from the Calcination is dissolved in the thoughtful meditations on the One, which continues throughout the Second Hermetic Discourse and the reading of the Gospel. The Dissolution concludes with the Act of Faith. At this point, the dross has been thoroughly exorcized, and all participants and celebrants are brought together under a single, inseparable consciousness and belief.

Let us proceed, then, with an examination of the Preliminary Rites:

Preliminary Rites

Since the celebration of our Liturgy of the Pleromic Light begins in the antechamber, that is to say the Pronaos of the Temple, let us begin there, by looking at the "Preliminary Rites" (*ACP Clergy Handbook* p. 166, or *ACP Lectionary for*

Mass, p. xii). The first instruction is to make the following invocation over the vestments:

"Our help is in the Name of the Lord. Bless these cloths and make for me a robe of Your Incorruptible Light. Amen."

The first words of this short prayer begin to reveal some of the particular theology of the Mass. It is a petition to "the Name of the Lord." This immediately tells us at least two things: 1st, that there is an inherent power residing in certain Divine Names; and 2nd, that it is "the Lord" to whom we petition. As a church of Christian Gnosis, the Lord that we beseech is of course Jesus, who is the central focus of the Eucharistic rite. But we must also mention here that it is the Holy Spirit that actually effects the transubstantiation; effects all of the sacraments of the Church, in fact. And in Gnostic theology the Holy Spirit is the feminine aspect of Deity. Thus, even though the Christian rites are filled with language and terminology that is principally masculine, even within the Gnostic churches (though they do offer much greater gender balance than the rites of the so-called orthodoxy), the Divine Feminine is ever-present throughout the Mass, whether visibly in the various symbolic elements, or invisibly as the directing power of the rite.

The concept of an exclusively male Trinity is not only in error, it has given rise to further errors, in an attempt to compensate for the obvious deficiency. Essentially what has been done by the Church of Rome is to feminize the Christ to the point that the Son has simultaneously become the consort of God the Father. And this relationship has been codified in the Creed through the addition of the controversial "*filioque.*" This refers to the procession, that is to say the emanation, of the Holy Spirit, which in the original Nicene Creed, rightly or wrongly, is said to proceed from the Father, but which was later changed in the Western Church to read "and the Son" (the meaning of the Latin *filioque*). Esoterically, this makes sense, at least if one insists upon an all-male Trinity, for it shows the creative process through the cooperation of polar elements, but this also places Christ firmly on the feminine side of the equation. This has even been reflected in the works of great mystics such as Jacob Bœhme and Papus; and in charts relating the Christian Trinity to the older Trinity of Father-Mother-Child, Christ is found in the "Mother" column, and the Holy Spirit in that of the Child. And this is all due to the "filioque" and to the notion of a strictly masculine Trinity.

To be sure, there is an androgynous quality to Jesus Christ, as a symbol of the reconciler, and the regenerated human. In fact, in the very Gnostic prologue to the "canonical" Gospel according to St. John, when discussing the incarnation of the Logos into the body of Jesus, it states, "in him was Life..."; that is to say Zoe, which, as Gnostics, we recognize as an aspect of the Aeon Sophia. Thus, in the person of Jesus is *both* the Logos *and* Zoe. It is only because of this embodiment of the perfect reintegration, that Jesus is able to be the type and the means to enable the union of our personal logos with Sophia, effecting our own restoration, and hers, into the Pleroma of Light. But to place the Christ in the position of the Mother is an error that has gone unrectified for far too long, and which may best be corrected, within the context of Christianity, through the adoption of a classical Gnostic theology, wherein the Holy Spirit, or Barbelo, takes her rightful place as Mother of the Aeons, and Christ, specifically the Logos, sits rightly as the Son, the Divine Child. But we can return to these topics later; let us proceed...

The vestments are transformed by this incantation, to "make for me a robe of your Incorruptible Light," from simple articles of clothing into a true spiritual armor. The style of vestment is not altogether important. Whether one vests in Byzantine, Roman, or Russian Orthodox attire, a pure white alb or jet-black cassock is really, in our tradition, up to the individual priest or bishop. Some sort of traditional ecclesiastical garb should be worn, as to be more easily recognized and assimilated by the egregore of the Church, and as many attributes of the office as possible (stole, pectoral cross, miter, crozier/litus, etc., etc.) should adorn the celebrant. But the style should really reflect the individual's personal connection to the office. The act of vesting is also a mental cue that a sacred rite is about to take place.

After vesting, an Acolyte enters the Temple and lights the Perpetual Luminary. The "Acolyte" here need not be currently of the rank of Acolyte (though this is preferable), but they should be *at least* of the rank of Acolyte. This action marks the first step in enlivening and "opening" the Temple. The Perpetual Luminary is representative of the Monad, the Celestial Fire of the alchemists. It is the primordial spark and source of all Divine radiance. All other fires emanate from this One Thing. It is the emblem of the Father of Light.

Upon the return of the Acolyte, the Thurifer goes into the Temple for a preliminary censing. The Thurifer should be of the rank of Exorcist, or, again, *at least* of the rank of Exorcist. In the system of the ACP, the Exorcist will likely have attained to the Martinist degree of Supérieur Inconnu in the Christian Knights of Saint-Martin. This is significant, as this preliminary censing is directly related to the occult currents of Martinism. The precise instructions for censing the Temple are found in the *Clergy Handbook* on pp. 160-162. But briefly, a sigil is traced out which is based upon the Martinist Pantacle, in the East, South, West, and North, with an arc of 90° connecting the center of one sigil to the center of the next. This circle of Fire and Air is emblematic of a much greater sphere of astral energy that will swell throughout the Mass as more and more spiritual essence is accumulated. This process of raising an astral edifice as a vehicle for spiritual power is described most beautifully and aptly by the late Archbishop Charles W. Leadbeater in his classic work, *The Science of the Sacraments,* which is required study material of all our Deacons in preparation for the Priesthood, which we

8

cannot recommend highly enough.

Once the Thurifer has returned from her duties, the Porter (or one who has attained at least that rank), as Conductor, calls the clergy to order by saying:

"My Brothers and Sisters come to order and prepare yourselves for our procession into the Temple of the Most High God."

At this call, the men and women of the clergy line up according to rank, silently. The Porter who is acting as Conductor, carrying the Sword, leads the procession, with the rest of the Porters behind him or her. Next follow the Lectors, headed by the principal Lector, carrying the Gospel aloft; then the Exorcists, the principal one acting as Crucifer, carrying the Cross into the sanctuary, which will be placed upon the Eucharistic Altar. One Exorcist will not be among this grouping, which is the one who acts as Thurifer, who will bring up the very rear of the procession. The Acolytes are lined up next, with the principal Acolyte bearing the Eucharistic elements upon a tray, that is to say the water and wine cruets, and the Ciborium filled with hosts; the Chalice, paten (with the priest's host), etc., will already have been placed upon the Eucharistic Altar by the Celebrant prior to these preliminary Rites. Next follow the Major Orders of Deacons, Priests, and Bishops. Visiting bishops are given a place of honor behind the bishops of the ACP. Then are the Eparchs (diocesan bishops), the Exarch, and the Patriarch; followed finally, as mentioned previously, by the exorcist who is acting as Thurifer. Not every celebration will necessarily have enough clergy present to fill every space denoted, and it would be perfectly acceptable to have the various liturgical items already placed within the Temple if there are not enough members present for the full procession. Though, the thurible should be carried into the Temple, even if it is by the Priest or Bishop himself.

Coming to order in this way is yet another mental cue that will further prepare those participating. The act of physically ordering the clergy can have the effect of helping to order the mind similarly, ensuring that all proceeds with regularity and a oneness of mind and purpose that will help open a strong and clear channel for Divine energy. And once everybody has settled into their position the principal Lector pronounces the Invocation of the Paraclete:

> "O Mother-Father of the Aeons,
> O Paraclete!
> Spirit of truth,
> Omnipresent and filling everything,
> Giver of Life!
> Come to dwell in us,
> Purify us of all iniquities
> And save our souls,
> O Merciful God!"

The clergy respond:

"Through our Lord Jesus, Christos, Soter, Logos. Amen."

This prayer contains the first overt reference in the Mass to a Masculine / Feminine polarity of the Divinity. In the Gnostic Scriptures, the Holy Spirit, or more specifically Barbelo, while being considered the feminine counterpart to the Father of Light, is also sometimes referred to as Mother-Father, or even Triple-Male! But we must remember that we are not talking about actual anthropomorphic beings here, but of spiritual entities that truly transcend any notion of gender. Thus, masculine attributes applied to an otherwise feminine deity merely indicates the incredible spiritual potency contained therein. Also, our mention of "God" throughout the Mass should not be seen as referring to "God the Father." In

10

our usage, "God" is a term that simultaneously refers to all three aspects of the Trinity working in concert toward one Divine aim and under one Divine Will. Some may also see in the term "Mother-Father" the pure, undivided Divine Essence.

The response to this prayer is found repeatedly throughout the Mass. Let us take just a moment to analyze these epithets of Jesus. First, he is called Lord. This is a title of nobility and mastership. By using this title, we acknowledge Him as our spiritual Master on earth. We look to Him as the exemplar *par excellence* of the Regenerated Human, restored to one's primitive rights, duties, and abilities. "Christos" means "anointed." This anointing takes place on multiple levels; first, there is the initial spiritual anointing by the Holy Spirit of the Logos; there is the anointing of his psychical body by Sophia as the Logos descends from the Pleroma into the Cosmos; and finally, there is his physical anointing. This anointing is sometimes related to his baptism by John, but although John is an important initiator here, it is not an anointing. If there is an anointing here at all it is a second pneumatic anointing by the Holy Spirit, or rather, it is the Holy Spirit recalling and activating the primitive anointing received in the Pleroma before his incarnation. But he does later receive a physical anointing by Mary. Just as Sophia is a type of Barbelo or the Holy Spirit in the Pleroma, then in the Psychical plane, the three Marys are too manifestations of this type on the physical plane.

"Soter" means "Savior." When we discuss soteriology, we are referring to the doctrine of salvation. Gnosticism does not have an "original sin" in the sense that the Roman Catholics mean it. The doctrine of original sin is based on the assumption that the human being is, from birth, fundamentally flawed, evil even; and that this defect must be removed at once through the sacrament of baptism, lest a child die in a state of sin. There are so many problems with this doctrine that it is difficult to know where to begin. Instead, let us look at the Gnostic view of sin and redemption. For the Gnostic, the only original sin is that of being in a state of unknowing. As opposed to the Roman Catholic view of the human condition, the Gnostic sees the human as fundamentally good, divine even. The only "sin" we bring into the world, and the sole cause of the errors we commit – errors that must, nevertheless be atoned for in some manner – is that of forgetting our origin and our true nature. Our need for a Savior or Redeemer, therefore, is not to change some fundamental part of our nature, but to help us remove from ourselves all that is *not* essential to our nature. It is through the gift of Holy Gnosis that the dark veils begin to lift, to reveal the true Pneumatic Light. And as concerns Baptism, we do not see it as some sort of divine triage performed on the floundering infant lest they slip into Hell's abyss. It is a powerful initiatory rite which, in my opinion, only holds real significance if it is undergone of one's own free will and accord, without any coercion or mental reservation whatsoever. And the Savior is the image of the Perfect Christian Initiate.

"Logos" means roughly "Word." In the Latin this is translated as "Verbum," and in the French as "Verbe." But in English we do not ever use the term "verb" outside of grammatical jargon, although we do use variants such as "verbal" or "verbage," etc. However, in the Latin and French we get a better idea of the "Word" in its state of activity as opposed to a mere static existence. The Logos is a driving, motive force; it is the Will of God put into action and manifestation. We read that all things were created through the Logos. This is not to say that the Logos personally created each thing individually, but rather that the force of the Logos is necessary to every creative process. Philosophically, the Logos also represents the reasoning faculties, thus the logos in the human being is the seat of consciousness.

Finally, the Name of Jesus himself is a great and powerful mystery. The name "Jesus," though powerful in its own right through centuries of use, is really a stand-in, a substitute word, so to speak, for the Hebrew יהשוה, the great and mysterious Pentagrammaton, or 5-lettered name. The mystery of the Pentagrammaton is a high occult teaching, and one to which we shall return further on in this analysis, when we reach the "First Hermetic Discourse"; and later put into practice in the "Theurgical Consecration." This invocation, then, of "Lord Jesus, Christos, Soter, Logos," is a powerful and comprehensive calling to the multifaceted nature of Christ.

After this prayer, the officiating celebrant calls for a period of meditation. During this brief time, all of the clergy silently contemplate their unique role in the celebration of the Mystery of the Mass and open themselves to the guidance of the spiritual forces that direct the liturgy. The opening of oneself to these forces, and to the "Angel of the Mass," also helps to further bring all of the brothers and sisters into a single mind and purpose. After a few moments of meditation, the Porter/Conductor says:

"My Brothers and Sisters, let us now enter the Temple of the Most High with the reverence due the Sovereign Architect of All Worlds."

This is the final admonition before processing into the Temple proper. This statement informs everybody that this Temple is dedicated to the "Most High." This lets us know that the "Sovereign Architect" referred to is not the demiurgic fashioner of the lower worlds, but the Grand Designer, whose flawless plans are carried out only imperfectly, first by Sophia, and consequently by the Demiurge. This admonishment is another of the mental cues indicating to the psyche that an attitude of solemnity and reverential awe is to be adopted. Before proceeding to the Procession itself, let us first analyze the layout of the Temple:

Temple Layout

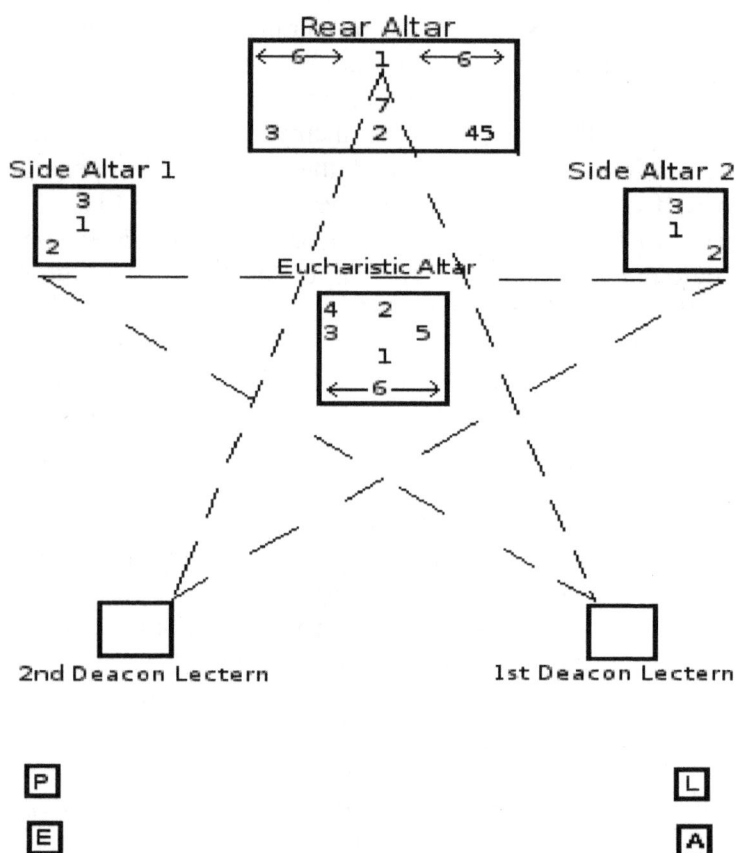

Rear Altar

←6→	1	←6→
	△	
3	/2\	45

Side Altar 1

3	
1	
2	

Eucharistic Altar

4	2	
3		5
	1	
	←6→	

Side Altar 2

	3
	1
	2

2nd Deacon Lectern

1st Deacon Lectern

P

E

L

A

Let us start with the over-all layout, and then move towards the various items found therein. The Temple is oriented East and West, so that the Rear Altar is in the East, etc. Geographical east is preferable, but the place of the Rear Altar is always considered as "East," sometimes called "Temple East." You will notice that the version included with this monograph has a pentagram inscribed over it, connecting the various altars and stations. This star does not actually appear in the Temple (although it could if so desired); it is merely included here to show its relation to the layout. The Pentagram has great occult significance, and has been used to represent variously: Woman (Venus in particular); Man; the Human form in general; the four elements: Fire, Water, Earth, and Air, with the addition of Spirit or Akasha; the Morning Star (Venus as Lucifer); the Evening Star (Venus as Vesper); the Human Will as agent of the Fall; the Human Will as agent of Redemption; and many other related significations, not the least of which is the aforementioned Pentagrammaton, the holy five-lettered name of Christ. The very shape of the Pentagram forms a sort of grid or network through which psychical and spiritual energy may flow.

Next, let us look at the positions of the celebrants, principally the Priest (who may be a priest or bishop) and the two Deacons, who are ideally ordained into the Diaconate; but this is not necessarily the case. Since the roles of 1st and 2nd Deacon do not require the performance of any sacramental function, these offices may be filled on a temporary basis by Minor Order clergy, or even by a lay person. They can, in fact, be dispensed with altogether if it is necessary, with the Priest reciting all the parts; or it may be performed with only one Deacon taking on both roles. But this liturgy is at its most efficacious when it is performed as designed. Just as the Eucharistic Altar falls within the center of the Pentagram, it also falls within the isosceles triangle formed by the priest and two Deacons. This arrangement of officers will be familiar to students and practitioners of continental – especially French –

15

Freemasonry, where the Venerable Master and his 1st and 2nd Surveillants are in precisely this position. Esoterically, there is a powerful dynamic established by this arrangement, and the various portions of tri-parted dialog serve to help raise the spiritual energy of the Mass.

Before looking at the spatial relations between the various altars, let us examine each of the tools of the Mass. Beginning with the Rear Altar, we have at the no. 1 position the seven-branched candelabra. This is a ritual item carried over from the Temple of Solomon. Its representations are so numerous, that an exhaustive analysis will not be given here. First, as stated in "The Alchemy of the Eucharist," just as the Perpetual Luminary represents the Celestial Fire, this item is characteristic of the Central Fire. To quote directly from this work:

Like the seven prismatic rays, it reminds us that the Logos of God is present within the core of all things. It is a goal common to both the Gnostic and the alchemist to release the inner essence that has been obscured by the darkness of matter. The number seven is also significant alchemically, because it represents the seven principal alchemical operations, which correspond to the seven planets of the ancients, as well as the seven metals.

The number seven is so prevalent in esoteric doctrine, that a practically endless list of correspondences could be given; the book of Revelation alone is filled with, and even based upon, this number. Let us move on...

At no. 2 is positioned the Lectionary. The *ACP Lectionary for Mass* contains all of the official readings for the standard Liturgical Year. The ACP has conformed itself, to a limited degree, to the Anglican and Roman Catholic cycles of readings. We have adopted a three-year cycle, wherein Year A is focused upon Matthew's Gospel, Year B upon that of Mark, and Year C upon that of Luke, with John being

16

interspersed throughout. Many of our Epistle and Gospel readings coincide with other Western branches of the Christian Church or are at least very close. This helps the ACP to participate in the powerful egregore established by the Church, as well as to offer her own insights and energies to that egregore with an aim towards eventual rectification. All of our New Testament readings, however, have been translated freshly from the Greek, using the *Greek New Testament* (UBS4) and the *Novum Testamentum Graece et Latine* (Ed. XXVII). This new translation has allowed us to preserve much of the esoteric and even specifically Gnostic language occurring in the original Greek, which, through ignorance or deception, has been overlooked or omitted in most mainstream translations. Additionally, we have excised nearly all Old Testament readings and replaced them with readings from the classical Gnostic scriptures. It is not that the ACP has abandoned the Old Testament in its entirety, for there is truly much of value to be found therein. But so much of it is tainted with Demiurgic doctrine and, in our opinion, human error, that we have chosen not to utilize it, for the most part, within our Lectionary readings, so as not to invoke any more of the Demiurgic influence than is absolutely necessary to the transubstantiation. There is a certain Demiurgic quality to the Eucharist, to be sure, the nature of which is outlined in "The Devil's Passion," found in the *ACP Clergy Handbook*. But we feel that the Demiurgic qualities are something to be acknowledged without necessarily being extolled. The replacement of the OT writings with the traditional Gnostic texts also gives a systematic exposure to these important works. Moreover, it has been mandated by the egregore of the ACP, and it is always best to give her what she wants...

At position 3 is placed the Thurible with the incense boat. The thurible represents the elements of Fire and Air, for obvious reasons. Concerning the alchemical significance it is the Elementary Fire, which is a destructive force. But esoterically we may read "destructive" as "transformative."

Without the destructive – the transformative – force of the hot coal, the essence of the incense could not be released. Historically, and poetically, the incense is seen to carry the prayers aloft to the presence of the Almighty. Watching the smoke rise from the thurible, with its whisps and curls and plumes, can be an entrancing experience. And the aromas that it carries can transport our consciousness outside of space and time. Various different incenses have traditionally been considered to produce different effects on one's consciousness, and upon the environment in general, aiding in the ease with which spiritual energies and entities may enter the sacred space. In the ACP, our standard liturgical incense is a blend of 2 parts Frankincense, 1 part Myrrh, and ½ part Sumatran Benzoin. This mixture, based on the formulas given by the late Gnostic Patriarch, and the namesake of the Mother Parish of the ACP, Robert Ambelain, has been found to provide an ideal commingling of masculine and feminine scents, so as to produce not a *balance*, which would be *static*, but a *dynamic* interaction, drawing and exciting the energies being raised.

At the 4 and 5 positions are the Aspergillum and Lavabo Font. Both of these *vessels* contain blessed Salt and Water, mixed. As the Thurible is representative of Fire and Air, the Holy Water is an emblem of Earth and Water. Both of these tools are used as a means of purification. The specific uses thereof will be addressed later, when their use appears within the Mass. But the relationship here between the Holy Water, Thurible, and Candelabra is worthy of further comment. This is a very old and traditional arrangement of an altar of high theurgy; and even though it is not the operational altar, it is a focal point and accumulator of spiritual energy that is drawn through the Celebrant and towards the Chalice.

To either side of the Candelabra may be placed various icons or other pertinent representations. These can be of Saints, Archangels, or even diagrams of an esoteric significance; perhaps even ancient stele or some other image or object. These items are optional and at the discretion of the

Celebrant.

Finally, in the center of the Rear Altar, is the Sword. This Sword, for certain esoteric reasons, is placed with its tip to the North. The Sword, while not used frequently liturgically, is nevertheless an important and traditional symbol. It recalls to us first of all the idea of a spiritual knighthood. It is an emblem of protection; but it is also an emblem of war. The Gnostic Priest must be a master theurgist; and as such is ever ready to not only come to the spiritual defense of one's fellow men and women, but also to bring the fight to the forces of spiritual darkness that seek to ensnare the soul, enchain the mind, confound the senses, and generally disorient the individual until there is no longer a sense of what is truth or falsehood. The Sword is a tool of *separation*; of dividing a thing into its consituent parts, whether it is in the alchemical laboratory or through the use of one's reason as applied to the liberal arts and sciences. The sword has many significations, and it is a worthy subject of meditation.

The two small altars to the North-West and South-West of the Rear Altar are attributed to Fire and Water respectively. The relationship mentioned previously, concerning the Thurible, Holy Water, and Candelabra, becomes extended by the Side Altars, with the Candelabra remaining as the apex of the triangle. But whereas the elemental representation in the first instance is related to Air, Water, and Fire, in the latter it become Fire, Water, and Spirit. Or, another way to look at this latter correspondence is alchemically; that is to say the *Gold* or Red Tincture (Fire), the *Silver* or White Tincture (Water), and the *Chrysopage* (Spirit). In any case, it is important to see the general relationship here, not to assign a very narrowly defined correspondence. When working with such pure spiritual powers as those evoked by the Mass, we are dealing in the realm of types or archetypes. So, the correspondences given are really only in order to help conceive of the *relationship* between the various elements, not to try to dictate a rigid and

19

dogmatic set of correspondences.

On Side Altar 1, that of Fire, is found the Perpetual Luminary. This is the light that was lit by the Acolyte just after vesting. It represents the primordial Celestial Fire; the Aesch of the Qabalists and Hermetic Philosophers. Also upon this altar may be found icons, statues, or other pertinent items. For example, an image or statue of the Archangel Michael would be most appropriate here. Also, if there are any special or occasional items, such as Holy Chrism, or any other item relating to Fire, it would be fitting to place it upon this altar until needed.

The Side Altar 2, or Water Altar, principally holds the Water and Wine cruets for the Eucharist. While the Water and Wine have a special polar complement to one another, they are both liquids, so, in a broader sense, both related to the Water archetype. Just as with the Fire Altar, images, icons, etc., are apt here; perhaps a representation of the Archangel Gabriel, especially if Michael is on the Fire Altar. And as before, this altar may also hold occasional items, such as Baptismal water, or any sacramental item related to the element of Water.

This brings us, then, to the Eucharistic Altar. This is the operative workstation of the Priest, and where the magic happens, so to speak. The centerpiece of the Altar, and of the entire Sanctuary, the veritable Holy of Holies, is the Chalice. The importance placed upon this ritual tool, ostensibly representative of the cup that held the wine at the Last Supper, while certainly being the case, harkens to an infinitely more ancient tradition which holds the vessel to be a representation of the Divine Feminine, the Cosmic Womb from which all emerges. It is the Grail of Barbelo and of Sophia, as well as of Mary; it is the primordial Bythos of the Valentinians. It is intended to contain the Blood of Christ; and it truly does. But Christ, like every child, receives his blood directly from his Mother. It is, therefore, and must be, the Blood of the Mother before it is the Blood of the Son. This Blood, whether actual blood, or sea water, or the ethereal Spirit, is the Vital and Universal Life Force. The Chalice is the Holy Grail of legend, the cauldron of the ancient witches, and the athanor of the alchemists.

Upon this sacred Chalice rests the Paten, a small indented disc, holding the Eucharistic bread which will be the sacrificial Host. The Paten, in a way, is but an extension of the Chalice; even though it is nearly flat, it is still a vessel of sorts. The Chalice, Paten, etc., are all covered by a Veil, indicating that this is truly the Holy of Holies that only the Priest may enter. More will be said on these items further on in our examination, when they are being handled in the Mass. The Chalice and its accouterments rest upon the Altar Stone, which is a traditional furnishing of the Eucharistic Altar, and which often contains within it a relic or relics of some Saint. It may also be engraved, for example, with the Seal of the ACP, or the Martinist Pantacle, or with some other appropriate design.

In the number 2 position is a copy of the Gospels, opened to the beginning of the Gospel according to St. John. It is no secret that this is common practice within the Lodges of Freemasonry, Martinism, and certain branches of the Rose+Croix. This Gospel is not the one that is to be read from during the mass, that is what the Lectionary is for. It is merely an emblem of the presence of the Word – that is to say the Logos – of God. In this respect it shares a relationship to the seven-branched Candelabra on the Rear Altar. This is the volume that is held high by the Lector during the Procession, the Lectionary already being in place. While this item may not seem to have much of a ritual use within the Mass – much like the Sword – it is nevertheless very important that it not be omitted. It acts as an attractive force to some very specific spiritual powers and entities who are particularly inclined towards our work, and who will recognize this emblem immediately. It is a cue to them, as is the general arrangement of the temple, that we are assembled to preform a ceremony of high spiritual significance. Now, every Mass is, of course, of a high spiritual significance, and there are certain entities that will come to attend and assist at every Mass. But parallel to this, our Temple represents a chamber of High Theurgy, which attracts an entirely different class of beings in addition to, and in complementary concert with, the usual Angels, Saints, and other spiritual beings that are attracted to the Eucharistic celebration.

In the third position is the Priest's ceremonial Dagger. Some also choose to lay the Dagger over the Gospel. If this is done, its point should be to the North, as the Sword. The Dagger is a symbol of the element Air according to tradition. Its primary use in the Mass is during the Invocation of the Archangels, during which every participant, clergy or not, may and should use their own Dagger, specially consecrated to liturgical and theurgical work; and during the Theurgical Consecration, by the priest alone. The style of Dagger is relatively unimportant, as long as its bearer is able to see it as a true tool of high theurgy. Simple or ornate, the Dagger should become an extension of the will of the celebrant, participant, or theurgist.

In the fourth place is the Bell. This is a traditional liturgical tool, and another whose usage goes very far back into antiquity. Its use is quite limited in the Mass, and I would not qualify it as an *essential* item; but it makes for a valuable addition if possible.

On the other side of the Chalice, at position 5, is the Ciborium. The Ciborium is a vessel that holds the communion wafers – other than that of the Priest, which remains upon the Paten – that are to be consecrated and transubstantiated into the Body of Christ. In most altar sets, the Ciborium is a nearly exact replica of the Chalice but having a lid or cover. It is not always the case that they match in this way and is by no means necessary; but it is often a nice touch.

Finally, along the western side of the Eucharistic Altar are placed icons or other significant representations, with the

Altar Cross in the Center. I find a Rose-Cross to be ideal, but this is not necessary. The style and size of the Cross should be left to the Priest and clergy. The one piece of advice here would be to consider using the Crucifix only during the Easter Season. The image of Christ Crucified, of the Dying God, certainly has a place within the Christian Church, even Gnostic Christianity; but the mysteries of death are only one part of the broader tradition, which in its totality is centered principally around Light and Life. The 365-day cycle of grovelling guiltily before an ever-suffering Savior is held by most Gnostics to be unhealthy, and frankly ridiculous. The Cross, to the Gnostic, and to the mystic and occultist in general, is so much greater than a mere tool of torture and execution. The Cross is an incredibly ancient symbol, found within the spiritual traditions of nearly every culture in every part of the world, to the North, South, East, and West. It is, among other things, the union of positive and negative, or rather masculine and feminine forces; and when set into motion it represents the whorling flames of the Sun and its life-giving rays. The tau, the equal-armed cross, the ankh or *crux ansata*, and other renditions are all symbols appropriate as the centerpiece of this Eucharistic Altar, and are all worthy of profound meditation and contemplation, and of our deepest respect.

Between the laity and the celebrating clergy are seated the Minor Order clergy. They shall, for the most part, respond along with the congregation. They are also "on call" however, for whatever service may be required of them during the Mass, such as holding the Missal, keeping a lit charcoal ready in the Thurible, pouring the Water and Wine into the Chalice, performing certain readings, etc., etc. These duties should be pre-arranged before the start of the Mass so that there is no confusion, and that the operation may proceed smoothly and naturally. Note too that while the Congregation faces East, the Minor Order clergy are seated facing each other, to the North and South.

Procession

With this introduction to the layout of the Temple complete, let us continue with the Procession of Clergy into the Temple. Let us quote the instructions given in the text of the Mass in full:

The clergy processes single file into the Temple, circumambulating the Eucharistic Altar three times clockwise. On the first circuit, the Holy Bible is placed on the Altar open to the Gospel According to John. On the second circuit, the Altar Cross is placed in position. On the third circuit, the Eucharistic elements are placed on their appropriate altars. After the third circuit, the clergy lines up a few feet in front of the Eucharistic Altar. However, the Porter bearing the Sword remains standing centered behind the clergy line; and the Exorcist who is acting as Thurifer stands directly behind the Porter, continuing to swing the thurible from side to side while the opening invocations are recited.

The circling of the altar is the first step in expanding the sphere initially created by the Thurifer during the Preliminary Rites. According to tradition, the clockwise motion produces an expansive force, whereas the counterclockwise movement contracts, draws in. There is a counterclockwise movement utilized in the Mass later on, and we will address it then. But here we are concerned with the inflation of the Gnostic spiritual sphere. Leadbeater, in his *Science of the Sacraments*, depicts this astral edifice as resembling a grand cathedral, replete with towering spires and soaring arches. This is a fine and useful visualization if it suits the individual. Personally, I tend towards the images that are simplest without losing their efficacy. Leadbeater was a very visually oriented mystic, so such images were very natural for him to sense and maintain throughout the Mass. For someone with such abilities, the image may be as rich and detailed as one can comfortably imagine without straining oneself to the point of distraction. For myself, I am more audio oriented than visual, so that hypnotic rhythms or an ethereal melody can do more to help me imagine the swelling of the sacred space than a pictorial visualization. Even the words of the Mass are a sort of music, whose cadence and intonation, when well delivered, can transport the speaker and hearer alike into a realm of mystical attunement, and can cause the soul itself to pulsate and grow with spiritual energy, pushing the boundaries of the sanctuary ever outward in all directions. And it is this omnidirectional growth and expanse that leads me to the concept of the sphere as being most appropriate. In fact, I would probably even argue that if one does wish to visualize a cathedral-type edifice, that they also visualize it being contained within a sphere.

When the clergy lines up before the Eucharistic Altar, I always find it preferably to have the officiating Priest (who, as stated previously, may also be of the rank of bishop, the designation of "Priest" here relating to the office filled in the Mass; just as this may be either a man or a woman, the term "Priest" here being intended as a gender-neutral term) standing in the very center, with the 1st and 2nd Deacon to either side. This, of course, is not the order of procession, but with a little practice, and everybody knowing their station beforehand, it can be carried out without too much disruption. This is, though, optional. Also, if there were a situation where a great number of clergy were present, it would also be acceptable to form the clergy into two rows before the altar. The Sword-bearer would then stand behind this second line. The Porter carrying the Sword should hold it before him or her, with both hands, the hilt at the level of the navel or solar plexus, the blade upright. The Thurifer swings the thurible slowly from left to right alternately in wide arcs. There should have been placed in the thurible a generous quantity of incense shortly before the procession, so that the fumigations may last throughout the opening invocations.

Invocation of the Aeons

Once all of the clergy are settled in place before the Altar, leaving enough room to advance by three steps and to kneel, the "Invocation of the Aeons" begins with the Priest making this announcement:

"In the Name of the Lord of all Worlds."

This announces to all, clergy and congregants alike, in whose name this liturgy is to be operated. It also reminds one of the phrase in the Noble Qur'an, "the Lord of the Alamin," meaning precisely the same thing, that is, Lord of all realms, of the living and the dead, of the Angels, Archangels, etc.

At this announcement the Priest and the 1st and 2nd Deacons – along with the rest of the clergy if it is desired – place their right hand over the heart. This is a universally recognized sign of fidelity. Additionally, this and the following signs have a certain mystical and secret significance which will be recognized by some, but which cannot be discussed in this public discourse. The Priest and Deacons, while maintaining this posture, intone I-A-O. The Priest begins by intoning the I (EE), followed by the 1st Deacon who intones A (AH), and the 2nd Deacon intoning O (OH). They are intoned in a way that the initial "I" is held for the whole duration of the three tones, so that all three: I, A, and O, end up being intoned simultaneously. There is not a precise amount of time that these intonations should be drawn out, but as a general rule, the 1st Deacon would begin the "A" about four seconds into the Priest's "I"; then after about another four seconds, the 2nd Deacon begins the "O"; and all three tones are held then for about eight more seconds. The Priest, therefore, must regulate his intonation so that it can be held

26

for approximately sixteen seconds.

The method for performing these intonations and the significance of each of the vowel sounds is addressed at length in the *Clergy Handbook* (pp. 151-154); but let us look very briefly at each of these intoned sounds. First, the purpose of mystical intonation is to establish a vibratory resonance within oneself and one's environment, with higher astral and spiritual realms. This is an application of the occult law of Correspondence, which holds that non-physical states can be affected by establishing a complement on the physical, sensory plane, using certain sounds, colors, scents, shapes, and even tastes. These intonations are intended to affect certain energy centers within the body of not only the one intoning, but also those within the immediate vicinity. These energy centers are what is known as "chakras" in Eastern mysticism. There are other methods of energy working, utilizing the classical "meridian" system, or more recent innovations such as the "point-chaud" or hot-point method pioneered by Bishop Michael-Paul Bertiaux and further developed by Bishop T Allen Greenfield and more recently by +Palamas, Gnostic Bishop and author of works such as *Syzygy* and *Spirit Builders*, which works specifically with the point-chaud method within the Gnostic-spiritualistic rite of Memphis+Misraim. But here we are concerned primarily with the seven principal energy centers; actually, only the upper four for this particular operation.

With the I-A-O intonation, then, the I should resonate at the Ajna or "third eye" region; the A at the Anahata or "heart/chest" region; and the O at Vishuddha or the "throat." Our experimentation has shown the net effect of this intonation to be, as stated in the *Clergy Handbook*, "the building up and focusing of the spiritual principle."

After these initial intonations, the Priest and Deacons (and other clergy if desired) place their hands, right over left, over the Solar Plexus. The intonation which follows is intoned approximately one or two octaves higher and is: I-A-UM.

27

This second triple intonation is performed similarly to the first, with the Priest intoning the first sound of "I" followed by the 1st Deacon with A, and the 2nd Deacon with the UM. The I and A here, although of a higher octave, should still resonate in the same physical regions as the I and A above. The "U" (OO) portion of the UM should be felt in the same place as the "O" above; but as the 2nd Deacon moves to the "M" sound, it should rise up to the Sahasrara region, which is at the top, or crown of the head. The effect here should be of focusing the spiritual power, as previously, then releasing it or emanating or radiating it from the top of the head.

The final triad of tones is: A-U-M. The posture to maintain for this is to have the arms crossed over the chest, right over left, palms open. This position is sometimes known as the Sign of the Good Shepherd. The sounds are intoned precisely as the first two sets, but at a tone lower than the initial IAO intonation. Here, the same order is followed: Priest, A; 1st Deacon, U; 2nd Deacon, M. And here the vibrations are moving straight up, from the heart, to the throat, through the top of the head. This intonation, according to the *Clergy Handbook*, "links the core of the individual with the macrocosm of the universe." All of these vowel-sound intonations are placed under the heading of "Invocation of the Aeons" because they are dealing with archetypal principles. These sounds, among others, and the energies that they activate are of an incredibly ancient and primitive origin. They hearken back to humanity's earliest utterances, holding a meaning only attached to the natural relationship between the sound and the force, not yet being confused by any syntax, grammar, or other elements that we today consider as "language." But it is a language nevertheless, a language of the spirit and the soul, just as much as the various polygonal shapes that would eventually differentiate into the written language.

When these intonations have concluded, the clergy place their hands together before them, palm to palm, as if in prayer. This is an ancient posture that was known in the East long before the advent of Christianity. It is known under a variety of terms, such as the prayer mudhra, or the namaste gassho, or any number of other designations. But the posture itself is instantly recognizable by all as one of reverence. This position is maintained during the three steps by which the clergy advances to the altar.

The "Prayer" position assumed, the Priest declares: "Lord of the Past," to which the Deacons and Priest as well (and the other clergy if desired) respond, "We hail thee!" During this response, all take one step forward, in unison, left foot first, bringing the right parallel with the left. The Priest continues, "Lord of the Present," followed by the same response, "We hail thee!" and the same single step forward in unison. The Priest makes the third proclamation: "Lord of the Future," followed again with the same response, and the third and final step. At this point, all kneel together before the Eucharistic Altar, on both knees. Kneeling is a sign of respect, humility, and submission to a superior will. But it is no human nor human will to whom we submit, but to the Divine Will and to the holy emblems of Divinity placed upon the Altar. It is in this position that we give glory to the Great Architect, and that our purpose is firmly declared, in these words:

"O Ineffable Light, Father of Resplendent Glory, Mother of Eternal Wisdom, we, being assembled together on the path of Light to manifest the Power of the Logos, the Christ within, and to participate in the offering of that great sacrifice which was, and is, and is to come, do hail Thee as the Great Architect of the Universe, and the Source of all Light, Life, Love, and Liberty."

In both the advancement to the Altar, and in the opening prayer, we are struck with a sense of timelessness; initially by reference to the Lord of the Past, Present, and Future, and then in reference to "that great sacrifice which was, and is, and is to come." The Mystery that we are celebrating is not only of all time, but in fact altogether outside of time. This is truly the nature of the Eternal. Having no beginning and no ending, It cannot have any sort of linear existence, since It is the very Source of our linear spacetime. Even spacetime is not really linear, in the way that it appears to our senses and our conscious awareness; how much less of its Source! It is this timelessness that we are entering into every time we celebrate the Holy Eucharist. And it is because of this timelessness that we are able to participate really and truly in the Body and Blood of Christ, and effect a true transubstantiation. We are not merely recreating a moment, we are actually experiencing that very moment from within the trans-spacetime sphere that we are building. All truly spiritual work operates outside of spacetime, and ritual, in this case the Mass, is our spacetime-traveling apparatus.

At this point the clergy rise and go to their stations. The Porter/Sword-bearer and the Thurifer go to the Rear Altar, where the first lays the Sword, pointing North, and the latter replaces the thurible at its place. The 1st and 2nd Deacons and the Priest assume their places; any additional bishops, priests, and deacons present may be given a place of honor, if there is room, at the East of the Temple, to the sides of the Rear Altar or between the Side Altars and the 1st and 2nd Deacons; or a special place may be arranged for them among the Congregation. These arrangements will vary depending upon the space available. The Porter/Sword-bearer and Exorcist/Thurifer, after replacing the items, join the other Minor Order clergy in the appointed place.

Once everyone has settled into their place and is prepared to continue, the Priest proceeds with the following prayer:

"In the Name of the Unknown One who reveals His Mysteries out of the Treasuries of Light to them that call upon Him, and who mercifully bestows His Secrets of Gnosis upon us without measure."

"May He always grant to us, through Christ the Eternal Logos, and the Divine Sophia, the revealer of His Gnosis, his eternal blessings that we may worthily preform the mysteries of the Mass. Help us to reveal the greatest Secrets which are lawful for man to know, and use them without offense unto God. Amen."

In this prayer, the "Unknown One" refers to the aspect of God that we typically refer to as the Father; sometimes referred to as the Unknown Father of Light. But this designation of "Father" or "He" is not to be thought of as a sort of anthropomorphic being, or of having any sort of gender as we might conceive of it. The term "Unknown" is actually quite apt. This Supreme expression of Deity, of which only negative terminology is truly appropriate (unknown, ineffable, limitless, etc.) is considered "masculine" only in the sense of its active, emanating power. In this sense, the Holy Spirit could be considered "masculine" as well, and is really only "feminine" relative to the "Father." Indeed, as we have seen, the Holy Spirit is commonly referred to as Mother-Father. An argument could possibly even be made to reverse these polar identities, but that, for us, would be an exercise in futility. Using the terms "He" and "She" are simply for our ease of use, and to try to help us get some small grasp, if not on the nature of Deity, at least on the relationship between the manifest attributes of Deity. And although we do not believe in an anthropomorphic God (that is to say, absolute Deity) it can be very useful to utilize anthropomorphic images in our conception; this allows us to identify with an incomprehensible Power at an intimate level.

The Treasury of Light is something we see referenced in the *Pistis Sophia*, and refers to the Pleroma – the Spiritual Fullness. Since the Mysteries are of the Pleroma, it is only through the bestowal of the Pleromic Light that we may gain an intimate Knowledge of those Mysteries. This intimate knowledge are the "Secrets of Gnosis" mentioned here, and they are truly a mercy, for without receiving them as a Divine Gift, we have no hope of attaining them. This is not an intellectual knowledge, though it is filtered through the intellect. It is more akin to an intuitive knowledge, yet it is far more precise and certain than normal intuition. But Gnosis, in order for it to be received and processed by the human being, must utilize the intuitive and intellectual faculties, though it is not a product of either.

We see reference then to the "Eternal Logos." We have discussed the concept of the Logos already, but we would just point out the use of "Eternal" here, indicating that the Logos is not something that came into being at the time of the physical Jesus, or even at the creation of the psychical Christ (see our "Devil's Passion" in the *Clergy Handbook* for more on this distinction); the Logos is coeternal with the Father and the Holy Spirit. We also see mentioned here, as if as a counterpart to the Logos, the "Divine Sophia." Now, although we do not recognize Sophia as equal to the Trinity, since she is not eternal, but an emanated Aeon, She is, nevertheless, divine, as are all of the Aeons of the Pleroma. And, according to our Gnostic tradition, it was with the Logos that She was intended to cooperate in her mission of creation. And despite Her failure to initially consummate that intimate union with the Logos, attempting instead to emanate from Her own essence alone, resulting in the imperfect matter and its lord, the demiurge, She is nevertheless a revered Divine being, Mother of all gods, and superior to every created thing. And it is now her unique mission to cooperate with the Logos towards the regeneration of humanity, and its reintegration into the Pleroma. As such, She is not only the revealer of the Gnosis of Christ, but even co-Redemptrix.

Finally, the Priest asks for aid in fulfilling his (or her) own mission of revealing "the greatest Secrets which are lawful for man to know." "Man" here, of course, refers to Humanity as a whole, not to some preferential status of the

Male gender, which, in fact, is only half of the primitive androgynous Anthropos, or Man. It has always been the duty of the priesthood of every true religion to help convey and interpret the will of God, and to teach others how to live in accordance with that will. The priesthoods have not always been successful in this, to be sure. At times, the priesthoods have lost their connection to the Divine Gnosis. Occasionally there have been those who have received the Gnosis, but communicated it insufficiently or improperly, or mixed with impure notions. That is why the petition is two-fold: 1) to reveal the Secrets; and 2) to "use them without offense unto God." The potential of the human will is an awesome and terrifying force. And these "greatest Secrets" concern precisely this topic; and its use may be to the greatest benefit of humanity and to the glory of God, or to one's utter detriment and ruin. The intentional misuse of spiritual powers is far worse than even one's former state of ignorance.

Next in the liturgy comes a brief dialog which precedes the lighting of the seven-branched candelabra. The Priest asks the 1st Deacon: "For what purpose do we congregate?" To which the Deacon responds: "To seek Truth." The Priest then directs his inquiry to the 2nd Deacon: "What shall we use to aid us in our search for Truth?" The 2nd Deacon answers, "The Light of Gnosis!" At this, the 2nd Deacon advances from her station to the Fire Altar (Side Altar 1) where she uses a thin white taper to draw a flame from the Perpetual Luminary. She (or he – I am using gender pronouns arbitrarily throughout) then hands the lit taper to the Priest, who proceeds with the lighting of the seven candles, starting with the center, then the one to the left, then that to the right of the center, and alternately left and right until all seven are lit. This is performed while reciting the following; the numbers indicate the lighting of each candle:

"O Pure Light! (1) Symbol of Divine Essence! (2) Light of the Empyrean Realm! (3) Make thy radiant and pure fire (4) purge and sanctify this (5), thy holy altar (6), and my lips (7) for the words that we are to proclaim for the greater glory of the Eternal. Amen."

The Priest, while continuing to face East, and holding the still lit taper in the right hand, arms outstretched, resumes the invocation:

"As these flames lighten our way in the earthly realm, so are the great Luminaries of the Aeons ever present to illumine and enlighten our spiritual path. Come, join us now, O great Luminaries; emissaries of the Most High!"

Now that the physical lights have been lit, the grand rulers of the Aeonic hosts themselves are about to be called forth into the midst of the sanctuary. These are the four chief Luminaries of the Aeons which appear in several Gnostic texts, such as the Apocryphon of John. To call them, their names are vibrated, intoned, similarly to the vowel sounds previously. These holy and divine names are now pronounced:

"HARMOZEL, OROIAEL, DAVEITHAI, ELELETH."

"Come now and witness as we praise the Most High, and prepare for the celebration of the most Holy Eucharist."

At this, the Priest extinguishes the taper *with the candle snuffer*, never blowing out the flame to extinguish it. This is a long-standing tradition within many esoteric orders and societies, and one that we feel important to preserve in the ACP. Remember that every word and action in the Mass should be significant; every gesture a representation of some principle. Here, the act of extinguishing the flame with the snuffer is emblematic of returning the flame to its point of original potential. That is to say that it is not to be viewed as a true "extinguishing" but as a change of state from active to inert. This Light, in its inert state, is ever ready to manifest at the call of the spiritual faithful. The act of blowing out a candle is seen, esoterically, as disrespecting the Light of Gnosis that it represents. This is a practice that many of us carry over to our profane lives, extinguishing every candle by a means of snuffing, thus treating every candle flame as a holy symbol.

The Priest then turns around to face the Eucharistic Altar, and begins a three-way dialog that is based, in part, on the prayer; "our help is in the name of the Lord, who made the heavens and the earth..." etc. Let us look at the whole interaction:

PRIEST: Our Help is in the Lord, secret center, heart and tongue.
1st DEACON: Whose Pure Will hath created worlds, and fitly framed the heavens hung.
PRIEST: Our Love is in the continuity of the Queen of Infinite Space.
2nd DEACON: Who from Her womb hath brought all things, yet knoweth neither time nor place.

Let us pause here to examine this first segment. Note first the pattern established here, from the Priest, to the 1st Deacon, back to the Priest, then to the 2nd Deacon. This sort of speech pattern, and other similar ones to follow a bit later, are reminiscent of certain Masonic or Masonic-type rites. This is, obviously, no accident. There are powerful occult laws at work within the Masonic Lodge, even, at times, without its participants being aware of them. The entire Lodge works as a machine, a generator of psychic and/or spiritual energy. The adornments, the placement and movements of the Officers, and their verbal interaction, are all working parts of this machine. The historical Eucharistic Liturgies work much in the same way. Within the Liturgy of the Pleromic Light, the ACP has endeavored to espouse the most effective of occult formulas in order to carry out its theurgical and sacramental mission. Additionally, the Church is bound intimately to the powerful egregores of Martinism and occult Freemasonry. These prayers and dialogs, therefore, are not at all arbitrary; but crucial and well calculated elements of a complex theurgical and sacramental formulary.

Next, we notice here a gender polarity at play, showing the complement of the "Lord" and the "Queen of Infinite Space." This refers simultaneously to the Unknown Father of Light and the Holy Spirit, as well as to the Logos and Sophia. This section is really a poetic depiction of the Hermetic point-within-the-circle, whose center is everywhere and circumference nowhere. We see this polarity continue in the following stanza:

PRIEST: Trust ye in the Pure Will.
1st DEACON: For He gives the Mind that understandeth.
PRIEST: Abide in the Love of Sophia forever.
2nd DEACON: For that Beauty is above comparison, and that Good is inimitable, as God Himself.

Here we have the complements of Will and Love, again poetically framed within a Hermetic context. One will notice a rather extensive utilization of classical Hermeticism throughout the Liturgy. The ACP recognizes the Hermetic Gnosis, though pre-Christian and "pagan," to be not only complementary to the Christian Gnosis, but in fact absolutely crucial to its full comprehension. This is not a recent innovation, for the presence of Hermetic texts among the Nag Hammadi texts suggests that they were in use as a part of the scriptural texts of the ancient Gnostics.

Returning, then, to the concepts of Will and Love, these should be seen as technical terms, illustrative of the creative and generative process. The Will is the masculine creative potency that sends forth the seed, be it thought or otherwise, toward the generative womb represented by Love.

Love, here, as the feminine counterpart to Will, is not merely a passive receptor. Once the seed has been received, it is actually the feminine principle that does the work of gestation, eventually bringing the resulting product into manifestation. So, it is wise to remember that the "feminine" pole is not merely "passive." It is the feminine principle that actually does the work of realization.

The dialog continues:

PRIEST: Blessed are the knowers of the Truth.
1st DEACON: For they shall ascend to the Light.
PRIEST: Blessed are those of the loving heart.
2nd DEACON: For Love and Truth will make them free.
PRIEST: The Truth and Love of God be with you.
CLERGY & CONGREGANTS: And with thy Spirit.

The "knowers" of Truth who "shall ascend to the Light," are of course the Gnostics. This knowing is such an intimate process, that it may be helpful to anthropomorphize Truth to an extent. When we think of Truth not as some mere abstraction, a concept of "factualness" but of an archetypal hypostasis, perhaps even under the Greek word of Aletheia, as an Aeon of the Pleroma, as an entity unto itself with which we may accomplish an intimate union, we may truly come to know Her bounty and Her fullness; Her transcendent essence which may truly transport us into the realm of Light and Life. The same may be said of Love, or Agape. These principles are so pure and lofty, that we commit no error in treating them as divine beings worthy of veneration, for they are truly a part of the "host of holy angels and messengers of Light" about which we are presently going to read. Which brings us to the close of this section, by the intoning of the Priest of the following:

"O glorious Godhead of the Aeons, Thou, secret center, Who art surrounded by the radiant presence of the host of holy angels and messengers of Light, hear our prayers and listen to our thoughts which rise from this world of shadows, toward Thy abode of unsearchable, unspeakable, and unending Light. Amen."

Invocation of the Archangels

This invocation is essentially an adaptation of the Lesser Banishing Ritual of the Pentagram, developed in the late 19th century by the Hermetic Order of the Golden Dawn. This rite has been adopted and adapted by dozens, if not hundreds, of esoteric bodies of every ilk, from Martinist Orders, to neo-pagan groups and heathen rites, to Thelemic bodies, etc., etc.; the adaptations of this rite are so frequent, so common-place, and whose source is so often uncredited, that many who utilize some form of this rite do not even know of its Hermetic Christian origin. Properly, it is a Qabalistic rite, as it makes use of the Hebrew God-names, as well as Archangelic names. Now, the original rite is called a "Banishing Ritual," but we have called it an "Invocation." In truth, it is really both. The "banishing" aspect of it is in the tracing of the "Banishing Pentagram of Earth," the purpose of which is to remove the lower-plane influences from the area. But as we know, Nature abhors a vacuum; so, the removal of the one type of influence is replaced by the invoking of the Archangelic influence.

In many adaptations of this rite, the Hebrew and the Archangels are replaced by other elements that correspond with the tradition making the adaptations, but the formula is always the same, and the general attributes are typically the same as well, making the particular names used somewhat arbitrary. I say somewhat, but not entirely arbitrary. There is certainly an effectiveness that resides in the formula alone, but there is also great power to be drawn in the proper intonation of these ancient names. We have made a few alterations to the original rite in adapting it for our use, but all of the original Names of Power have been preserved. The specific

38

instructions for the performance of the Invocation have been given in detail in the *Clergy Handbook*, but we will give a brief walk-through of the rite, as well as a few explanatory notes which, although pretty basic, do not appear in the *Clergy Handbook*.

The Priest announces to everybody, clergy and laity alike: "Please rise for the Invocation of the Archangels." At this, all rise and either participate in the ritual or remain standing silently during its performance. All begin, following the motions of the Priest as a cue, by making what is known as the Qabalistic Cross. The gestures are to make the sign of the cross in a manner similar to the Eastern style, that is to say by crossing from the right shoulder to the left, as opposed to the manner of the Roman Catholics, who cross from the left to the right. It is begun by facing East and saying "Ateh" (which is pronounced more like ah-tah) while touching the right index finger to the forehead, at the Ajna "third eye" position. A line is drawn straight down to below the naval while saying "Malkuth." The finger is brought up to the right shoulder, saying "Ve'Geburah," then crossed over to the left, saying "Ve'Gedulah." Then the hands are brought together in the so-called prayer mudhra or Namaste gassho (a term familiar to the initiates and practitioners of Migaku Reiki) to say, "Le Olam." The arms are then crossed over the body right over left, while A-U-M is intoned as discussed previously. But unlike in the opening intonations of the Mass, all three tones are pronounced by each person, they are not split into three parts. These words (except for the final intonation) are a transliteration of the Hebrew, meaning approximately: "Thine is the Kingdom, the Power, and the Glory forever." Our use of the A-U-M takes the place of the word "Amen" found in other versions of the Qabalistic Cross.

At this point, the ceremonial Dagger is drawn, or the index finger continues to be used. While still facing East, a large Pentagram is to be traced out in the air with the Dagger (or finger), beginning with the lower left angle, moving up to

39

the apex, back down to the lower right angle, and so on. It is common to visualize this star as glowing yellow, since that is the color commonly associated with this quarter. Additionally, it is associated with the element of air. After drawing this pentagram, the following is recited:

"In the Name of יהוה (Yod-He-Vav-He), we invoke thee, Archangel of the East, RAPHAEL!"

To make this invocation, both hands are brought to either side of the head, a deep inhalation is taken, the words "In the Name of" are pronounced; then a step is taken forward with the right foot only (as opposed to the left in some variants of this rite, including the original), at the same time that the arms are thrust forward. As this motion is made, the god Name Yod-He-Vav-He is intoned. The ACP's method of intoning the Names of God is very similar to that used by the Builders of the Adytum, an esoteric order founded by former Golden Dawn member Paul Foster Case. However, where the BOTA utilizes four separate tones for this first name, we typically intone it monotonally. The ACP is not, however, opposed to any of its members utilizing the multitoned form. The words "we invoke thee, Archangel of the East," are then declared forcefully, followed by the intonation of the Archangelic Name Raphael. Some people like to visualize the presence of the angel before them, sometimes accompanied by a sensation of blowing wind. The Archangel Raphael is often imagined as having yellow robes, the color corresponding to this direction, sometimes with purple accents, being the complementary color to yellow.

When the sound of the Archangelic Name is completed, the right foot is withdrawn to be parallel with the left, and the hands are brought down to the side. Then the hand holding the Dagger is raised to point at the center of the pentagram drawn in the air. With the Dagger extended, the body is rotated 90° clockwise to the South, thus drawing an

40

arc connecting the first pentagram to the next one which is going to be made. A pentagram is drawn here in the same manner as before, but may be visualized as glowing red. All of the motions are identical to the first invocation; this one proceeds:

"In the Name of אדני (Adonai), we invoke thee, Archangel of the South, MICHAEL!"

All of the previous comments apply to this invocation. I would note only that its associated color is red, whose complement is green; and the associated element is Fire. The Dagger is, again, pointed toward the center of the five-pointed star. And carried in an arc 90° to the West, where the star is drawn and visualized as glowing blue. Here is the Western invocation:

"In the Name of אהיה (Eheieh), we invoke thee, Archangel of the West, GABRIEL!"

The color for the West is blue with orange secondarily; the element is Water. Everything proceeds as before, turning to the North, and making the invocation:

"In the Name of אגלא (Agla), we invoke thee, Archangel of the North, AURIEL!"

The color associated with this last invocation is not universally agreed upon; or rather, there are acceptable variants. As it corresponds with the elements of Earth, in the ACP we utilize a dark, forest-green, with an earthy brown as its complement. These colors, and black, are all appropriate for visualizations.

Before coming to the conclusion of this section, a few words should be said on the "God names" used here. The first, in the East, is the Tetragrammaton, the holy and ineffable

41

four-lettered name. This name has long been considered to be unpronounceable in its true form. Therefore, the tradition has arisen to only spell the name, its true pronunciation having been lost. Thus, our pronunciation of the four Hebrew letters separately. There is so much that may be said on this name, that I hesitate in approaching the subject at all. Let us say briefly, that the Tetragrammaton is not simply a name, but an entire formula unto itself. Although it is composed of four letters, only the first three are unique, the fourth being a repetition of the second. We may thus draw a direct correlation between this trigram and our Holy Trinity; wherein the Yod corresponds to the Father, the He to the Holy Spirit, and the Vav to the Logos. The final He, being a type of the Holy Spirit, that is to say the Divine Mother, may be correlated to Sophia. In Qabalistic lore, the Divine equilibrium of the Tetragrammaton was said to be broken at the time of the Fall. This corresponds perfectly with our Gnostic mythos, where Sophia becomes trapped outside of the Pleroma, necessitating the descent of the Logos, which becomes enmeshed in the physical world for a time until the Pleroma can be restored. For more on this topic, please see our "The Tetragrammaton in the Three Worlds" which may be downloaded at pleromachurch.org. Etymologically, this name seems to be derived from the verb "to be."

The Name Adonai means "lord" and was used frequently as a stand-in for the Tetragrammaton. Nevertheless, through centuries of use, it has developed a certain power as a name in its own right. The early 20th century occultist Edward Alexander "Aleister" Crowley had a great fondness for this Name, and it appears in some of his channeled writings.

The Name Eheieh means roughly "I am that I am"; or sometimes it is simplified to "existence exists." Qabalistically, this is the God name associated with the highest sephirah on the Tree of Life, Kether. It also represents the foundation of all philosophy. Descarte may have said "cogito ergo sum," but behind this there has to be the acceptance of the very concept of existence as opposed to non-existence. Or, Qabalistically, it represents the first point of existence to coalesce from so-called "negative existence."

The final Name, Agla, is actually an acronym. It stands for the phrase: Ateh gabor le-olam adonai. Thine is the power forever, O Lord. This acronym, though, through its repeated use in esoteric and occult ritual, has become a potent Name, on par with any of the great Names of God of antiquity.

It is in the Names of Deity above that the great Archangels have been called to stand watch. The spiritual mass and might of these powerful guardians of the four quarters pushes the boundaries of the sphere of operation to a much greater extent. And the following rite of the Asperges continues this expansion even further.

Asperges

The term "Asperges" comes from the Latin *aspergere*, meaning "to sprinkle." This brief but all-important rite consists of the sprinkling of Holy Water to further purify the operational environment of the Mass. The sprinkling is performed while reciting the invocation which we shall presently give in full:

"Purify us, O Lord, that in Thy Power we may worthily perform the Great Work. In Thy strength, O Indwelling Lord, do we expel all forces of darkness from this, Thy Holy Altar and Sanctuary, and from this house and our own human temples wherein we worship Thee; and we pray Thee Heavenly Father, that Thou wilt command the Rulers of the Four Regions, your mighty Archangels, Lords of the Air, Water, Fire, and Earth, to build for us a Spiritual Temple through which Thy Strength and Blessing may be poured forth upon Thy people. Through Christ our Indwelling Lord."

All reply to this, "So mote it be!"

This sprinkling is directed first towards the Eucharistic Altar, three times to the center, three times to the left, and three times to the right. The Priest then turns around to face the Rear Altar and likewise sprinkles three times each to the center, left, and right. Then he sprinkles in a full 360° arc; there should be at least eight shakes of the aspergill; that is to say at least once at each eighth of the circle, but more is fine too. This purification, being of Salt and Water – that is to say Earth and Water – is very much a complement to the initial censing of the Temple at the very beginning. And with each shake of the aspergill, especially while making the circle, the operative sphere should be visualized as growing ever larger and ever stronger. Also, the Priest should endeavor, during these sprinklings, to make sure that some drops of the Holy Water land upon the members of the clergy and even into the congregation, as each particle of this water carries a powerful benediction. And the response of "So mote it be" will be familiar to Freemasons, Rosicrucians, and others, as meaning simply "let it be so." This is an archaic terminology, but has been used ritually for a very long time. Grammatically, it is similar to the French phrase "Ainsi soit-il," which is used in most classical French prayers and liturgies in place of "Amen."

Prayer

This prayer will be recognized at once by some ritualists as being an adaptation from the Key of Solomon. There have been some very minor alterations to these orisons to reflect its liturgical context, as well as to reflect better the particular theology of the ACP, but it has been left as close as possible to the original. Here is the text:

"When we enter herein with all humility, let God the Almighty One enter into this Sanctuary of the Gnosis by the entrance of an eternal happiness, of a Divine prosperity, of a perfect joy, of an abundant charity, and of an eternal salutation. Let all the demons fly from this place, especially those who are opposed unto this work, and let the Angels of Peace assist and protect this Sanctuary, from which let discord and strife fly and depart. Magnify and extend upon us, O Lord, Thy most Holy Name, and bless our conversation and our assembly. Sanctify, O Lord our God, our humble entry herein, Thou the Blessed and Holy One of the Eternal Ages! Amen."

"I beseech Thee, O Lord God, the All Powerful and the All Merciful, that Thou wilt deign to bless this Sanctuary, and all this place, and all those who are herein, and that Thou wilt grant unto us, who serve Thee, and rehearse nothing but the wonders of Thy Law, a good Angel for our Guardian, remove from us every adverse power; preserve us from evil and from trouble; grant, O Lord, that we may rest in this place in all safety, through Thee, O Lord, Who livest and reignest unto the Ages of Ages.

"O Lord God, All Powerful and All Merciful, Thou who desirest not the death of a sinner, but rather that he may turn from his ignorance and live; give and grant unto us Thy Grace, by +Blessing and +Consecrating this Altar and this Sanctuary, which is here marked out with the most powerful and holy Names of God. And may God bless this place with all the virtues of Heaven, so that no obscene or unclean spirit may have the power to enter into this Sanctuary, or to annoy any person who is therein; through our Lord Jesus, Christos, Soter, Logos, Who liveth eternally unto the Ages of Ages. Amen."

Some of the language found in these prayers and others to follow may seem somewhat out of place in a Gnostic liturgy at first glance, but one should always open oneself to the deeper significations of prayers and rites that seem more related to "orthodox" traditions than to our own. Additionally, these prayers, through centuries of ritual use, have developed a great power and efficacy that help the celebrant to connect oneself and the important work at hand to some of the most potent currents of High Theurgy. These prayers are not mere pleadings for grace and protection, they are among the very highest of occult incantations.

Censing of the Altar

The prior, pre-liturgy censing was to purify the Sanctuary in general, and to demark its initial boundaries. This censing is a purification of the Eucharistic Altar in particular. With the Asperges, the blessing and purifying by Water and Earth, both the Sanctuary and the Altar were included in the same rite. With the censing, the blessing and purification by Fire and Air, the process has been divided into separate rites. This censing is, therefore, directly connected to the initial censing, as its continuation and completion. While the Priest puts some incense into the thurible, it is blessed in the Name of the Trinity by saying: "Creature of incense, be thou blessed in the Name of the +Father, and of the +Son, and of the +Holy Spirit," making the Sign of the Cross over it at each +. The Priest then censes the Altar, center, left, and right, three times each, just as with the Asperges, while reciting these words:

"Purify this place, O Divine and Eternal One, and make of us one mystical Body, growing into the Pleroma of your Gnosis. Make us a Spiritual Temple of living stones, through which your infinite Light may flow. Let the Holy Angels of Light join with us, and assist us in this act of divine transformation. We unite now to celebrate, knowing that we all come from the Original Light, which is the Source of everything visible and invisible."

After this, the Priest replaces the thurible, or hands it off to an assistant to be replaced; then makes the Sign of the Cross over the clergy and congregants with the right hand in the sign of benediction, while saying: "May the Lord be with you." To which all respond: "And with thy spirit." Concerning this latter response, it is somewhat interesting to note that it was used for many years in the Roman Catholic Missal, but was discontinued after Vatican II, being replaced with the phrase, "And also with you." Over just the past few years this has been changed back to "And with your spirit," a form much more closely resembling the pre-Vatican II usage. It is also interesting that much of the Independent Catholic and Liberal Catholic movement has retained the older usage the whole time, as have many branches of the Gnostic Church, who share a good deal of common ancestry with the broader Independent Sacramental Movement, with which we also share a liturgical inheritance. There is an intricate web which connects independent churches and clergy across a vast and diverse span of theologies, yet united by the apostolic and sacramental tradition. On this topic, the reader is referred to the classic work by Peter Anson, *Bishops at Large*, which gives a fairly comprehensive, if biased, account of a large swath of the independent movement at the time of its writing in the 1960s. Also of note is John Plummer's brief but insightful and informative treatise, *The Many Paths of the Independent Sacramental Movement*.

Confiteor

The idea of confession is often not very popular among many of the independent sacramental churches, much less so among the Gnostic branches. This is largely because of what is considered to actually constitute "sin" and the desire not to fall into the cycles of perpetual guilt promulgated by some of the mainstream branches (and some independent branches, to be sure). But just as the perpetual guilt imposed by some is unhealthy and unproductive, and not conducive to spiritual growth, so too is the ignoring of one's faults detrimental to one's psychical and spiritual development. To feel guilty for some injustice that one has caused is a perfectly appropriate response. Between the extremes of wallowing in self-loathing and despair over every perceived imperfection, and an aloof and indifferent sociopathy that divorces one's psyche from one's actions and their consequences, is a healthy state of recognizing and acknowledging honestly one's shortcomings, imperfections, and outright failings. It is not necessary that one confess every fault to his brothers and sisters, or even to his priest or bishop (although this can have a cathartic effect for some), but one must, if one wishes to progress towards spiritual perfection, be entirely honest with oneself and with the spiritual forces that have the ability to provide corrective actions.

Our Confiteor is in two parts: a shorter section recited by all clergy and congregants, and a longer portion reserved for the Priest alone. Let us look at the first, public, recital:

"O Lord, that which is mortal cometh not into a body immortal; but that which is immortal cometh into that which is mortal. Thou art Thou, all that is made, and all that is not made. Thou art all things, and there is nothing else Thou art not. I beseech Thee that I may never err from the knowledge of Thee. For Thou art what I am, Thou art what I do, Thou art what I say. Amen."

This Hermetic-Gnostic confession acknowledges that there is but one substantial reality that underlies all manifestation. But it is only by the Light of Gnosis that we may recognize this fundamental unity behind the apparent multiplicity. When one is in this state of *Gnosis*, which is a state of perfect *Equilibrium*, one knows which actions are correct and which are in error. In this way, Gnosis – the aforementioned "Knowledge of Thee" – is the only true remedy for "sin."

Another aspect of this recital that should be addressed

Confiteor

briefly goes to a point of Gnostic doctrine; it is the opening sentence: "O Lord, that which is mortal cometh not into a body immortal; but that which is immortal cometh into that which is mortal." This shows us the path of descent, which is therefore the path of return. It tells us that the coarser may serve as an envelope for the finer, but not the other way. Thus, the Spirit requires a psychic envelope, as the psychic requires a hylic, in order to manifest below. To use an analogy of the physical realm, a liquid may be contained within a solid vessel, but a solid cannot be contained within a liquid; the solid merely displaces the liquid. This is not a precise analogy, but it is close. What we learn from this process of the descent of Spirit into matter is that we must shed the dross – that is to say the physical and the psychical – in order to return to the Pleroma, the realm of Spirit. In order to don the garment of the Body of Light, the Soul must wholly Spiritualize, for "that which is mortal cometh not into a body immortal."

The second, longer part of the Confiteor is that which is recited by the Priest alone:

"O Lord All Powerful, Eternal God and Father of ALL, Shed upon me the Divine Influence of Thy Mercy, for I am Thy Creature. I beseech Thee to defend me from mine enemies, and to confirm in me true and steadfast faith. O Lord, I commit my Body and my Soul unto Thee, seeing I put my trust in none beside Thee; it is on Thee alone that I rely. O Lord my God aid me. O Lord hear me in the day and hour wherein I shall invoke Thee. I pray Thee by Thy Mercy not to put me into oblivion, nor to remove me from Thee. O Lord be Thou my succor, Thou Who art the God of my salvation. O Lord make me a new heart according unto Thy loving Kindness. These, O Lord, are the gifts which I await from Thee, O my God and my Master, Thou who livest and reignest unto the Ages of the Ages. Amen."

"O Lord God the All Powerful One, who hast formed unto Thyself great and Ineffable Wisdom, and Co-Eternal with

49

Thyself before the countless Ages; Thou Who before the birth of Time hast created the Aeons, and the things that they contain, Thou who hast vivified all things by Thy Holy Breath, I praise Thee, I bless Thee, I adore Thee, and I glorify Thee. Be Thou propitious unto me who am but a miserable sinner, and despise me not; save me and succor me, even me the work of Thine hands. I conjure and entreat Thee by Thy Holy Name to banish from my Spirit the darkness of Ignorance, and to enlighten me with the Fire of Thy Wisdom; take away from me all evil desires, and let not my speech be as that of the foolish. O Thou, God the Living One, whose Glory, Honor, and Kingdom shall extend unto the Ages of Ages. Through our Lord Jesus, Christos, Soter, Logos. Amen."

Some of the language used above (e.g. "I pray Thee...not to put me into oblivion...who am but a miserable sinner..." etc.) does not really seem to fit within the Gnostic ideology. But there are, nevertheless, good reasons for including it here. First, the Priest is taking full responsibility for all the errors he has committed and is making every attempt to totally purge himself of all that is impure. A certain amount of self-effacing can be effective to this end. It can also be dangerous, because we do not actually want to damage the efficacy of the will, or to develop some unhealthy masochistic self-hatred. But under the right conditions and proper controls, it can indeed be an effective tool. Alchemically speaking, as pointed out in "Alchemy of the Eucharist," this is part of the "Calcination" phase, wherein the dross is purified. In fact, this Confiteor represents the very pinnacle of that phase. Here is where the alchemical furnace is at its very hottest, reducing the impurities to ash, revealing the pure First Matter with which the alchemist attempts her rectification, to produce the fabled Philosopher's Stone. And it is because of this "volatile" nature that this portion is reserved to the Priest alone. It must also be mentioned that these confessions of the Priest are adapted, like the prayers mentioned previously, from that classic occult tome, *The Key of Solomon.*

Absolution

The Absolution, in the so-called "orthodox" sense is the act of the Priest forgiving the sin of the penitent; literally obliterating the "sin" from their soul. To view the sacrament in this way is dangerous to the well-being of the faithful, detrimental to their spiritual evolution, and, from the Gnostic perspective, just plain erroneous. Now, a Roman Catholic Priest might give someone a penance, or expect them to feel remorseful, etc., but if they truly believe in the absolute efficacy of the sacraments, that the sacrament is performed by the Holy Spirit and is irrevocable, then according to their own doctrine, the "forgiven" or "absolved" individual will be so whether he or she feels remorse or not. I do not think I need to comment further on the absurdity of this notion. To the Gnostic, every error must be accounted for. In order to make spiritual progress, one must accept full responsibility for the free use of one's will. To attempt to alleviate that responsibility is to give up one's liberty of will. When the Gnostic Priest prays for the forgiveness of the congregation and clergy, he is not asking for a simple erasure of deeds and memory; he is invoking powerful spiritual aids that may help the individual to reconcile oneself with the Divinity. To this end, the Absolution of the ACP contains elements familiar to our more mainstream sister churches, as well as specifically Gnostic elements adapted from the *Pistis Sophia*:

"God the Father + God the Son + God the Holy Spirit + Bless + Strengthen + Preserve + and Sanctify + you. May the Lord in his loving kindness look down upon you that you may win the victory over your lower selves and receive the Grace and Comfort of the Holy Spirit."

"Hear me, O Father, father of all fatherhood. I invoke you, ye forgivers of sins, ye purifiers of iniquities. Forgive the sins of the souls of these disciples, and purify their iniquities and make them worthy to be reckoned with the Kingdom of the Father of the Treasury of the Light."

"Now, therefore, O Father, father of all fatherhood, let the forgivers of sins come, whose names are these:

"Σιφιρεψνιχευ ζενει βεριμου σοχαβριχηρ ευθαρι να ναι φιεισβαλμηριχ μευνιπος χιριε ενταιρ μουθιορ σμουρ πευχηρ οουσχους μινιονορ ισοχοβορθα."

"Hear me invoking you, forgive the sins of these souls and blot out their iniquities... Let them be worthy to be reckoned with the Kingdom of the Father of the Treasury of Light."

"I know the great powers and invoke them:"

"Αυηρ βεβρω αθρονι η ουρεφ η ωνε σουφεν κνιτουσοχρεωφ μαθωνβι μνεθωρ σουωνι χωχωετεωφ χωχε ετεωφ μεμωχ ανημφ."

"Forgive the sins of these souls, blot out their iniquities which they knowingly and unknowingly have committed; forgive them and make them worthy to be reckoned with the Kingdom of the Father, so that they are worthy to receive this Eucharistic Offering which we have come to make, Holy Father. Through our Lord Jesus, Christos, Soter, Logos. Amen."

"The Lord has put away all your sins. Abide in the peace and love of the Holy Spirit. Amen."

Again, despite some of the traditional language used here, such as "The Lord has put away all your sins," one should always bear in mind what was just said on this subject above. The cleansing of the soul is certainly possible, but the Priest simply helps to facilitate this process. Any proclamation by the Priest that one's sins have been forgiven or absolved is not a divine fiat, it is entirely contingent upon the individual having made the necessary atonements.

In the Roman Catholic Church, one may not partake of the Eucharistic elements if one is in a state of sin. This general absolution is typically seen as sufficient for eliminating so-called venal sin. There are scriptural bases for this practice, principally those laid out by Paul in 1 Corinthians which caution against receiving the Eucharist unworthily, least they "eat and drink judgment against themselves." There is truth in this, to be sure, as the Eucharist should never be consumed frivolously or without the deepest reverence and respect in one's heart.

But one does not have to be in a state of perfection in order to receive the Eucharist. Such is a ridiculous notion, for it is the Eucharist itself that helps to bring one closer to perfection. Someone who was truly "without sin" – that is to say in a state of complete spiritual awareness and equilibrium – would no longer have any need for the Eucharist, for it would have already served its ultimate function of regeneration and reintegration.

Sign of Peace

The Sign of Peace, or Kiss of Peace, is a traditional part of the Christian Eucharistic service. When practiced as the Kiss of Peace, some churches have the Priest give the kiss upon the forehead of the nearest assistant, which is then passed from person to person, through the clergy and the laity, until it is returned to the Priest. There are a number of variations on this practice, but even a simple handshake among the brothers and sisters creates a strong connection between all present. It is believed that certain energies are exchanged with human touch, and the intermingling of auras – energy fields – of the individuals helps to bring everybody together into a single will and purpose. The announcement for the Sign of Peace is as follows:

"My Brothers and Sisters in the Gnosis, the Lord of Agape binds us with a bond of Love that cannot be broken, Therefore we invoke the indwelling Christos, who does ever say the Thy disciples: 'Peace I leave with you, My peace I give unto you.' Grant us that peace and unity which are agreeable to Thy Holy Will and Commandment. In the Name of our Lord Jesus Christ, Savior and Logos, may the peace of the Lord be with you always."

First Hermetic Discourse
called Psalm of Wisdom and Praise

The Hermetic Discourses of our Liturgy serve to both instruct the mind and elevate the soul. These tri-parted narratives are adapted from the *Corpus Hermeticum*, the principal collection of Hermetic Scriptures. We view Hermetic Gnosticism and Christian Gnosticism to be essentially two sides of the same coin. The lessons of the Hermetic texts can greatly elucidate the fundamental Gnostic doctrine. It is my opinion that these texts are more useful as points of thoughtful contemplation and meditation than as subjects of critical analysis; but we shall say a few words regardless. Since this is a rather lengthy section, let us break it down bit by bit. Here is the opening, recited by the Priest:

"Which way shall I look when I praise Thee? Upward? Downward? Outward? Inward? For about Thee there is no manner, nor place, nor anything else of all things that are. But all things are in Thee; all things from Thee; Thou givest all things and takest nothing, for Thou hast all things and there is nothing that Thou hast not."

The first note to be made concerns certain gestures that are to be made here. During the words: "Upward? Downward? Outward? Inward?" The Priest should first raise his arms up, outstretched in a V shape, then down to his sides, but again out in a V shape, not parallel with the body; then the arms are lifted to the level of the shoulders, stretched out

54

horizontally, side to side; finally, the arms are brought to cross over the chest, right over left, in the Sign of the Good Shepherd discussed earlier.

Concerning the doctrine expounded here, there are really two points to be drawn herefrom, summed up in the statements: "...all things are in Thee; all things from Thee." The first part gives us a basis for our claim that Gnosticism – Christian, Hermetic, or otherwise – is panentheistic. That is to say that all things are contained within the Divine Immensity, though the Divinity Itself remains boundless. This differs from pantheism in that pantheism is something of a closed system; nature and nature's laws are essentially the constituent parts of the Deity; God and the Universe are seen as one. In panentheism, while all of the manifest universe is contained within the Deity, the Deity Itself is not constrained by it; It is both immanent, being the very substantial reality through which everything moves and acts and exists, and transcendent, existing both within and without. The second part, "all things from Thee," lays the foundation for the doctrine of emanation; that is to say the act of creation by an "issuing forth." The doctrine of emanation is fundamental to Hermeticism, Qabalah, and Gnosticism. Let us continue, then, with the next part, which is recited by the 1st Deacon:

"He that shall learn and study the things that are, and how they are ordered and governed, and by whom, and for what cause, or to what end, will acknowledge thanks to the Great Architect. And he that gives thanks shall be of the Spirit. And he that is of the Spirit shall know both where the Truth is and what it is; and learning that, he will be yet more and more of the Spirit."

In good Hermetic fashion, this section shows how the study of Nature (in the classical sense of natural philosophy, physics, etc.) may lead to spiritual awareness; or how a study of the Monad leads to a study of the Absolute. This is a form of inductive reasoning which allows us to make suppositions about the General, based on the knowledge of particulars. Our Hermetic author here is certain that an investigation into the nature of things will lead one to an Absolute Cause. Now, it is interesting to read that, "he that gives thanks shall be of the Spirit." This would suggest that the act of thanksgiving is much more than a simple acknowledgment; there is even a very beautiful Hermetic "Prayer of Thanksgiving" included among the Nag Hammadi texts, which was undoubtedly used ritually or sacramentally. The word "Eucharist" itself comes from a Greek word meaning grateful or thankful. Giving thanks is therefore one of the spiritual keys to accessing the Gnostic realms, for we read further that, "he that is of the Spirit shall know both where the Truth is and what it is." The Truth, Aletheia, is nothing less than a high Aeon of the Pleroma; and to truly know her is indeed to be "yet more and more of the Spirit."

The 2nd Deacon continues:

"For never shall or can that soul which, while it is in the body, lightens and lifts up itself to know and comprehend that which is Good and True, slide back to the contrary; for it is infinitely enamored thereof and forgetteth all evils; and when it hath learned and known its Father and Progenitor, it can no more apostatize or depart from that Good. That which is Good desireth to be set at liberty; but the things that are Evil love slavery."

This passage tells us that true salvation comes through Gnosis; that, enlightened by Holy Truth, the soul itself becomes Good. That is to say that the psychical nature becomes spiritualized. And once this state has been attained, once the soul, the seat of consciousness, has connected intimately with the true inner spiritual essence, that it is forever changed by that experience, and is no longer able to partake of anything of the lower natures. There is, however,

First Hermetic Discourse

and unfortunately, an exception to this rule that is not spoken of frequently, but when it is, it is spoken of strongly. It is the notion of the blaspheme of the Holy Spirit, the so-called "unforgivable sin." This is not merely some invention of the Christian orthodoxy, it is addressed within the canonical New Testament as well as within multiple Gnostic texts. We have addressed this topic elsewhere, such as in our essay "Theosis Through Gnosis," as well as in homilies delivered to the Parish of St. Ambelain, so I do not wish to linger too long upon this topic; but it is something worth addressing at least briefly. I think it should suffice here to repeat what is stated in the *Clergy Handbook* (pp. 23-24) on the topic:

Those who have attained to the Light of Gnosis but have turned away from that knowledge and have willfully returned to a state of darkness and ignorance will not be allowed to regain gnosis through successive incarnations. According to the Secret Book of John, *these unfortunate souls "will be taken to the place where the angels of misery go, where there is no repentance. They will be kept there until the day when those who have blasphemed against the Spirit will be tortured and punished eternally.*

A little further on, the *Handbook* cites the *Pistis Sophia* on this topic:

All men who shall receive the mysteries of the Ineffable – blessed indeed are the souls which shall receive of those mysteries; but if they turn and transgress and come out of the body before they have repented, the judgment of those men is sorer than all the judgments, and it is exceedingly violent, even if those souls are new and it is their first time coming into the world. They will not return to the changes of the bodies from that hour onwards and will not be able to do anything, but they will be cast out into the outer darkness and perish and be non-existent forever.

57

These are grim words, to be sure, but it goes to illustrate the point that gnosis is so precious and so holy, that to do the unthinkable, to reject one's very means of salvation, is to be considered as the very gravest of all errors. It is difficult, in fact, to imagine how something like this could even happen, but the fact it is mentioned and dealt with multiple times, among different theological schools, tells us that we should consider it as a real phenomenon, and that we should guard and cherish every glimpse of the Holy Gnosis, and that we must take to heart the lessons it imparts to us.

As we move on to the next section of this "Discourse," we return once more to the well-known Hermetic image of the point within the circle; making plain here what was alluded to earlier in the Mass. Here is the exchange between the Priest and the Deacons:

PRIEST: I give praise and blessing to God the Father.
1st DEACON: Who art everywhere the center of the sphere.
PRIEST: I give praise and blessing to the Mighty Mother.
2nd DEACON: Whose circumference is nowhere found.

The relationship shown here between the masculine and feminine aspects of Deity is very interesting. One is tempted to see herein that the immanence of Deity is the masculine and that the feminine represents the transcendence. Yet, to insist upon this in an absolute sense would only be a half-truth, for surely the Holy Spirit may be experienced immanently, and surely too there is a transcendence to the Unknown Father of Light. These dichotomies are only to be reconciled through contemplation and meditation. But we nevertheless see in this simple but beautiful image the intimate and dynamic interaction between the polar aspects of Divinity, which is utterly necessary to the process of manifestation. Let us read further, in the next section, about the fruit of this interaction:

PRIEST: Wisdom is to be understood in silence, and the Seed
    is the true Good, sown by the Will of God.
1st DEACON: The Child of God is the Author of Regeneration.
    The One Man by the Will of God.
2nd DEACON: Things of this kind are not taught, but are by
    God, to whom he pleaseth, brought to remembrance.

The initial words of the Priest, that "Wisdom is to be
understood in silence," reinforces what we have said about the
necessity of contemplation and meditation for the attainment
of gnosis. We see here also a dichotomy or polarity
established between Wisdom and "the Seed" which is "the
true Good." With little effort, we may translate this Hermetic
terminology into Gnostic terminology and read Sophia and
the Logos. In Qabalistic terms, the Father and Mother spoken
of in the previous section are the ' and the ח, while the Logos
and Sophia – the Seed and Wisdom – are the ו and the final ח.
Thus, we have not merely a second binary, but a quaternary.
    The line spoken by the 1st Deacon refers, of course, to
the Christ himself. When we read "the Child of God" we may
indeed read this as "Child of the Pleroma," for it was through
the cooperation of the Fullness of the Divine Aeons that the
Savior, the "Author of Regeneration" could be made manifest
here on earth. Though it is true that in Jesus Christ is the very
essence of the Logos made manifest, it is more accurately the
Logos united with Sophia, in the form of Zoe – life – that has
ultimately manifested; for remember that John's Gospel tells
us that "in him was Life [Zoe]." This is what differentiates the
advent of Christ from a former descent of the Logos, which
was merely the impersonal creative power or "energy" of the
Logos, whereas in Christ is the very "essence" of the Logos,
equilibrated by Zoe, and thus an equilibrating force himself.
Qabalistically he is represented by the letter ש (Shin), wherein
we may discern a composite hieroglyph of the whole
Tetragrammaton. The ש is also the mediating factor that
reconciles the fractured Pleroma, uniting the logos in man

with Sophia, and restoring both to the Pleroma, whose fracturing we represented earlier as the separation between the יה and the וה of the Tetragrammaton. Christ, as the Reconciler, forms a new Name, the Holy Pentagrammaton: יהשוה. The mysteries of this Name, rendered in the common tongue as Jesus, are many. We have just summarized its principal import, but its practical and revelatory value is only to be fully grasped individually, though gnosis.

The words of the 2nd Deacon address this very concept of gnosis. The language used by the Hermetic texts to describe gnosis as something that is "not taught" but "brought to remembrance," describes perfectly the gnostic sensation experienced by so many. The process of gnostic revelation often feels like a distant memory is being awakened which, after remembered, one realizes was known all along, but merely forgotten. It has the sensation of something familiar returning, not of something new and strange. The 2nd Deacon's words also indicate that this remembrance is given "by God, to whom he pleaseth." This is indicative of a sort of spiritual election; but it is not an arbitrary election. The treasures of the Pleroma are bestowed only upon those found worthy, it is true, but this worth is not found by any external measure, neither by bloodline nor rank or station among one's peers. It is the result of an inner preparedness that may be discerned only by the high and holy Beings of the Pleroma.

The final portion of this Discourse is dedicated to acknowledging the might and holiness of the Divinity. Here are the final recitations:

PRIEST: I give praise and blessing unto the One.
1st DEACON: Holy is God whose Will is performed and accomplished by his own powers.
2nd DEACON: Holy is God that determineth to be known and is known of His, or those that are His.
PRIEST & DEACONS:
Holy art Thou, that by Thy Word hast established all

things.

Holy art Thou, of Whom all Nature is the image.

Holy art Thou, Whom Nature hath not formed.

Holy art Thou, that art stronger than all power.

Holy art Thou, that art greater than all excellency.

Holy art Thou, Who art better than all praise.

O Thou unspeakable, unutterable, be praised with silence!

After this final declaration, all the clergy and laity observe a few moments of silent reflection. This final series of statements, Holy art Thou...etc., should be emphatic, building up an intensity that is all the more punctuated by the silence which follows. This type of ritual performance is not commonly seen in modern Christian liturgies. But it was likely quite common in the Gnostic liturgies of the first centuries of this era. Many Gnostic writings are full of ritual glossolalia, sacred dances, and other elements that one might more readily associate with pagan rituals than with Christian ones. But such is the Gnostic heritage. The ancient Gnostics were never shy about their syncretization of the older pagan traditions with the new revelations of the Christos, which they believed to be a natural extension, the one from the other. Nor should we deny our rich and varied inheritance. Some of the early Church Fathers sought a supposedly pure Christian gnosis, separated from any non-Christian or pre-Christian pagan elements. Many of them made worthy attempts and did indeed contribute to certain notions popular among today's mystical Christian sects, such as Origen's doctrine of universal redemption. However, the ACP is not merely mystical, but truly Gnostic, in the classical sense. And while we certainly appreciate the many contributions towards the mystical philosophy that have come from within the so-called orthodoxy, we honor and practice the same sort of syncretism that so notably marked the writings and practices of our forebears of antiquity. And although our rites may not be identical to those of the ancients, their spirit is certainly the same.

First Reading

A quick glance through the *ACP Lectionary For Mass* will reveal that nearly every "First Reading" is from one of the classical Gnostic texts. Now, scholars may argue whether the *Odes of Solomon* or the *Gospel of Thomas* are properly Gnostic, but such minute academic distinctions ought not concern us. The various classifications of the scholars are educated guesses at best, in some cases probably entirely arbitrary or even erroneous. The early heresiologists seemed to often invent their own classifications of the "Gnostics" of the day, and the academic community seems to be happy to fulfill that role in our day. This is not meant to be disparaging towards the many excellent academic efforts that have been made in the field of Gnostic scholarship. I just do not think that we need to let those outside of the tradition define it for us. To the practicing Gnostic, to the one who has actually experienced Gnostic revelation, the "Gnostic" quality of a text has less to do with whether the Demiurge or certain Aeons are mentioned, than if the text reflects certain principles and notions that have the hallmarks of Gnostic revelation.

After the First Reading, the Priest says:

"Give ear unto us, O Indwelling One, while we sing Thy Praises. Thou Mystery before all uncontainables and impassibles, Who did shine forth in Thy Mystery, in order that the Mystery that is from the beginning be completed in us, Here us, O Father of boundless Light, Mother of Eternal Wisdom! All has come forth from Thee, and will return unto Thee, when the consummation of all consummations has taken place. Amen."

Second Hermetic Discourse
called The Secret Song

We note first that the recitative order of this Discourse is different than anything we have encountered up to this point in the liturgy. The order now begins with the 2nd Deacon, goes to the 1st Deacon, then finally to the Priest, and so on. This begins to move the flow of energy in the opposite direction; counter-clockwise. We mentioned previously that, according to tradition – and, we might add, verified by personal experimentation – the clockwise motion tends to expand, whereas the counter-clockwise tends to contract. So, by reversing the direction here, it is not that we are contracting or shrinking our sphere of operation, but we are drawing in the spiritual energies that have been accumulated within this sphere. Remember, that the Eucharistic Altar is the focus of our operation, and that the Chalice, along with the Paten, is the focal point of the Eucharistic Altar. Although the Eucharistic transubstantiation has not yet begun, this "drawing in" is helping to coalesce the spiritual energies around the Altar, so that at the time of the consecration of the Eucharistic elements, these energies will come rushing into them. Let us examine this "Discourse" then as we did the previous one, taking one "stanza" at a time:

2nd DEACON: Let all the Nature of the World entertain the hearing of this Hymn.

1st DEACON: Praise ye the Lord of the Creation, and the All, and the One; the Name of the Most High be praised.

PRIEST: Let us altogether give him blessing which rideth upon the heavens; the Creator of all Nature. This is he that is the eye of the mind, and will accept the praise of my powers.

We must be clear here that the appellation of "Lord of

the Creation" does not refer to the demiurgic lord of the lower worlds, but to the architect of the grand design, of which the Demiurge's handiwork is but an imperfect model. This is made clear here by reference to the "Name of the Most High." We also see, in reference to the "All, and the One," not only familiar Gnostic terms, but another depiction of the point-within-the-circle; therefore, although the pronoun "he" is used, there is a veiled acknowledgment of both the masculine and the feminine aspects of Deity. It is important to be able to identify this polar complementarity in mystical writings, for if they are genuine, then it *must* be there in one form or another. This is likewise true when we see feminine-centric texts such as the Gnostic treatise *Thunder: Perfect Mind*. Without complementarity there is no union, and without union there is no manifestation. Let us continue reading the next part:

2nd DEACON: O all ye powers that are in me, praise the One and the All.
1st DEACON: Sing together with my will, all you powers that are in me.
PRIEST: O Holy Knowledge, being enlightened by thee I magnify the intelligible Light, and rejoice in the joy of the Lord. By me the Truth sings praise to the Truth, the Good praiseth the Good. O Life, O Light, from us unto you comes this Praise and Thanksgiving.

In these beautiful phrases we see again the Fullness of God addressed and adored. In the lines of the 2nd Deacon we are taken back again to the notion, common to both Hermeticism and Gnosticism, of the One (point/immanence) and the All (circle/transcendence). The Priest sings the praises of the Holy Gnosis itself. It is interesting to note that the Hermetic author has made a point of indicating the *intelligible* Light, that is to say the Light that may be known, as opposed to the ineffable, unknowable Light, which cannot even be approached, let alone "magnified." This sentiment hearkens back to the notion appearing near the beginning of the Mass of revealing "the greatest Secrets which are lawful for man to know." The "Lord" mentioned here should be understood as the Christ. And the Life and Light are yet another example of the complementary forces. These are particularly known to Gnosticism and to Christianity in general. I am, at this moment, looking down at the pendant hanging around my neck, which is an equal-armed cross, with the Greek words ΦΩΣ and ΖΩΗ (phos=light, zoe=life) appearing vertically and horizontally respectively. The polar complementarity here therefore refers to that which exists within Christ himself, for recall that "in Him was Life" and that we also read from the same text that He is "the Light of the world." This Life and Light is therefore emblematic of Zoe and the Logos united in the person of Jesus Christ. Finally, the Priest brings us back to the idea of Thanksgiving. It is peculiar, and unfortunate, that the concept of Thanksgiving, so central a theme among the Hermetic scriptures, is so little discussed when considering "Hermetic Philosophy." When we consider the principal role that the notion of Thanksgiving plays among the Hermetic writings, it becomes evident that the Eucharistic service is a most appropriate place for the exposition of the Hermetic doctrine. Let us continue with the next section:

2nd DEACON: I give thanks to Thee, the Operation of my powers.
PRIEST & DEACONS: A-U-M.
1st DEACON: I give thanks to Thee, the Power of my operations.
PRIEST & DEACONS: A-U-M.
PRIEST: By me Thy Word sings praise unto Thee. Receive by me this verbal sacrifice.
PRIEST & DEACONS: A-U-M.

In the first line, pronounced by the 2nd Deacon, is giving thanks to the Feminine aspect of Deity. Remember that it is the Mother who gestates and makes manifest. In this case, the "Operation" refers to the making manifest of one's will, or "powers." The line spoken by the 1st Deacon is, consequently, giving thanks to the Masculine aspect; the "Power" is the Divine Will that we seek to manifest here below through our gestative "operations." The words of the Priest acknowledge that it is the power (that is to say the active force) of the Logos within oneself that is actually effecting the Thanksgiving. Finally, the A-U-M intoned in between each of these lines, with the arms crossed in the "Good Shepherd" position, links, as stated previously, the core of the individual with the Macrocosm; or the "point" with the "circumference." The final tri-partition is as follows:

2nd DEACON: The powers that are in me cry these things, they praise the All, they fulfill Thy Will; Thy Will and Counsel is from Thee unto Thee.

1st DEACON: O All, receive a reasonable sacrifice from all things; O Life save all that is in us; O Light, enlighten, for the Mind guideth the Word.

PRIEST: Thou art God, Thy child crieth these things unto thee, by the Fire, by the Air, by the Earth, by the Water, by the Spirit, by Thy Creatures.

PRIEST & DEACONS: So Mote It Be!

Given what we have said regarding the various terminology used throughout the Hermetic Discourses, the reader may easily analyze for herself the various dynamic interactions of Hermetic principles here. This section ends the Hermetic Discourse proper. What follows, from this point up to the Epistle, is not technically part of the Discourse, but has not been given its own heading (though perhaps it should have been). The next section is adapted from the Gospel of Philip. It consists of the following call and response between the Priest and the rest of the clergy and laity.

V./ Faith is our Earth in which we take root.
R./ Amen.
V./ Hope is the Water with which we are nourished.
R./ Amen.
V./ Love is the Air through which we grow.
R./ Amen.
V./ Knowledge is the Light by which we ripen.
R./ Amen.

Our "Brief Analysis of the ACP Seal," available for download from the ACP website, discusses this a little bit, as the passage from the Gospel of Philip informs, in part, the construction of the Seal of the Church. Let us take just a short time here to quickly review the elements of this passage. There are two main elements to be noticed here. The first is that we see the three theological virtues, Faith, Hope, and Love (sometimes called Charity, but this is not quite right, for the Greek *Agape* is Love, which in Latin was translated as *caritas*, from where comes the word *Charity*), with the addition of Knowledge, that is to say *Gnosis*. Secondly, each of these is correlated to one of the four elements. This correspondence is what has informed the placement of the four words in the arms of the Cross of the ACP Seal, to wit:

Αγαπη (Agape = Love) is in the upper arm of the Cross which, in this Seal, represents the *East*, which is traditionally associated with the element of *Air*;

Γνωσις (Gnosis = Knowledge) is upon the right-hand arm representative of the *South*, associated with *Fire*;

Ελπις (Elpis = Hope) is in the lower arm, the place of the *West*, associated with *Water;*

Πιστις (Pistis = Faith), finally, is in the *North*, which is associated with the element of *Earth*.

This entire segment is closed by the Priest reciting the following:

"It is Christ who standeth at the door of every heart. Open ye your heart unto Him that ye may be One. For as the

67

One is in the All, so is the All in the One. Thus the Logos sayeth: As I am One with the Father, so ye are One with me. Then may ye enter that Supernal Sphere, and dwell in that great celestial mansion whose pillars are: WISDOM, STRENGTH, and BEAUTY."

We have discussed already the notion of the One within the All, as being illustrated as the point within the circle; a boundless circle, to be sure, so that every point therein is the true center. Here, we are now introduced to the idea that the All is also in the One. We may think of this as similar to a hologram, where the entire image is contained within every portion. In this case, it is the fullness of the Pleroma, or at least its image, that is contained within everything. This may also be compared to DNA, the genetic code, which is present in full within each of the cells, even though the cells be specialized. This follows the Hermetic axiom of "As above, so below," or better "as *within*, so *without*." The Gnostic Scriptures tell us as much, that the "uppermost" is the "innermost." And the Supernal Sphere mentioned here is none other than the Pleromic realm, which at the level of the Microcosm is to be understood as the state of perfect equilibrium. The three pillars named will be familiar to every Mason and Martinist. Their names can be derived from certain Sephiroth of the Tree of Life, namely the 2nd (Chokhmah = Wisdom), 5th (Geburah = Strength), and 6th (Tiphareth = Beauty), and each of these pillars represents the column on the Tree of Life wherein each Sephirah is found. (See Appendices B and C in the *Clergy Handbook*, or any number of Qabalistic treatises.)

At the conclusion of the above recitation, the bell is rung three times by the Priest. Alternatively, if there is no bell present, the Priest may give three raps, equally spaced, upon the Eucharistic Altar with the handle of the Dagger. After the chime of the bell has waned, the Priest and the two Deacons intone "Amen."

Epistle

The Epistle, also called the *Lesson*, is (usually) the second reading from the Lectionary. The heading here is "Epistle" but the Second Lectionary Reading may also come from the *Acts of the Apostles* or *Revelation*, neither of which actually qualify as an epistle. Also, at the Feast of Pentecost, which is the anniversary of the establishment of the Church in a general sense, as well as of the ACP in particular, *The Folly of Peter* is read in its entirety. The Epistle is commonly read by the Lector, but any of the clergy, even one of the laity, may perform this reading. At the end of the Epistle, or Second Reading, the reader states: "Here endeth the Lesson"; to which all respond: "Thanks be to God."

Gradual

The Gradual is a very traditional reading between the Epistle and the Gospel. The word comes from the Latin *gradus*, meaning "step." The only real difference to be found in our version of the Gradual from many others is that we have utilized the personification of Wisdom – Sophia – not only to bring it into closer alignment with Gnosticism, but to emphasize the intimate relationship we are to have with Her. This "change" is really barely a change at all, as the personification already exists in the text; we have merely used the Greek word. And although we have not rendered "Life" as "Zoe," the implication is there none-the-less. Here, then, is the text of the Gradual, recited by the Priest:

"He that loveth the Holy Sophia loveth Life; and they that seek her early shall be filled with Joy.

Teach me, O Lord, the way of Thy statutes, and I shall keep it unto the end. Give me understanding, and I shall keep Thy law; yea I shall keep it with my whole heart. The path of the just is as the shining light, shining more and more unto the perfect day."

Munda Cor Meum

This is another very traditional liturgical recitation which occurs before the reading of the Gospel. The words "Munda cor meum," are simply the Latin for the first words of the reading, "Cleanse my heart..." The important thing to note here is that the "Deacon" who says this portion, and who is to perform the reading of the Gospel, must actually be of the rank of the Diaconate or higher. The reader of the Gospel may be, therefore, the 1st or 2nd Deacon, provided that they actually hold the office, or the Priest, or another non-celebrating member of the clergy who is present, and who has attained to the Diaconate. The Deacon who is to read the Gospel recites the following:

"Cleanse my heart and lips, O God, who by the hands of Thy Seraph didst cleanse the lips of Thy prophet Isaiah with a burning coal from Thine altar, and in Thy loving kindness, so purify me that I may worthily proclaim Thy Holy Gospel. Through Christ, our Indwelling Lord. Amen."

Next, the Priest blesses the Deacon with the following words:

"May the Lord be in thy heart and on thy lips, that through thy heart the love of God may shine forth, and through thy lips His power be made manifest. Amen."

Gospel

The reading of the Gospel is a sacred and solemn ceremony, carried out by all apostolic churches with the greatest reverence. The fact that we are a Gnostic Church does not in any way diminish the esteem that we hold for the canonical Gospels. The goal of Gnosticism has never been, in nearly all cases, to refute or undermine the canonical tradition, but to supplement, augment, and expound upon it with a continued revelation. It elaborates and elucidates the messages of the Spirit hidden within the Gospel, which may only be properly understood within a Gnostic context. As mentioned previously, the *ACP Lectionary For Mass* follows the 3-year model set by the Western Churches, so that Year A focuses on *Matthew,* Year B on *Mark*, and Year C on *Luke*, with John's Gospel interspersed throughout the three liturgical years. The ACP has utilized the outline proposed by the Consultation on Common Texts in their *Revised Common Lectionary* as a basis upon which to construct its own Lectionary.

The Deacon Proclaims: "Please rise for the reading of the Gospel." When everyone is standing, she says, "The Lord be with you," to which all respond, "And with thy spirit." Then as the Deacon announces the Gospel to be read, she makes the sign of the cross with the right thumb successively upon the forehead, lips, and heart. The clergy and laity alike respond: "Glory be to Thee, O Lord."

Before the reading of the Gospel commences, the Deacon censes the Gospel in the usual manner, three times each at the center, left, and right. For this censing the Lectionary should be open to the proper reading. The Gospel is then read by the Deacon. The reading of the Epistle and the Gospel are traditionally performed at the South and North sides of the Eucharistic Altar respectively, though some may prefer to perform all the readings before the Eucharistic Altar. The ACP leaves this to the discretion of the chief celebrant, though it should be decided beforehand so as not to cause any confusion or disruption during the Eucharistic service.

At the conclusion of the Gospel reading, the Deacon says, "Here endeth the Gospel"; to which all respond: "Praise be to Thee, O Christ." Then the Deacon gives a final admonishment, taken from the Epistle of James (1:22), but which is sadly lacking in many modern liturgies: "Be ye doers of the Word, and not hearers only." The Deacon then has everyone retake their seats and censes the Priest. This concludes the ceremony of the reading of the Gospel. It is followed by the delivery of the homily by the Priest or some other designated speaker, as well as any announcements or the performance of Baptisms or other ceremonies.

Act of Faith

The Act of Faith is essentially the Creed of the ACP. It lays out some of the principal tenets of the Gnostic theology of the ACP. It begins by the Priest declaring: "Please all join me in the Act of Faith." Then everyone recites, while placing the right hand over the heart, the following:

"I believe in the Ineffable, Unknowable Father, incorruptible Spirit, Lord of All Worlds, Architect of all things visible and invisible. Light of Light."

"And in the Pure Will of the Father which sends forth the Seed, which is the true Good. Life of Life."

"And I believe in the Holy Spirit, Sublime Mother of the Aeons, from whose womb all things are made manifest and to which they shall return. Love of Love."

"And I believe in the incarnation of our Lord Jesus Christ, self-generated and alone begotten; creative essence of the Father; Logos of the Eternal Aeon; the Author of Regeneration, through which we may loosen the bonds of matter and recall our own divine nature, and become one in the fullness of God. Liberty of Liberty."

"And I believe in the communion of the Holy Saints and Prophets."

"And I believe in the miracle of the Eucharist, whereby the elements of Bread and Wine are transmuted into the Body and Blood of Christ the Logos, giving us Spiritual sustenance, and a visible means of grace."

"And I believe in One Universal and Apostolic Church of Light, Life, Love, and Liberty."

"A-U-M A-U-M A-U-M."

There is much said in these several lines, so let us go through it bit by bit. You will notice that all of the concepts presented here are present throughout the Mass. Looking at the first section, we see reference to the Unknown Father of Light. The designation of "Lord of All Worlds" is used at the very beginning of the Mass, where we have already discussed it. Likewise, the designation of "Architect" occurs early on and is found repeatedly throughout the Mass. The designation of "Father" is perhaps somewhat of a misnomer, since the designation of "Unknown" truly supersedes all other appellations at this stage of Divine manifestation; it is actually as yet unmanifest. But we nevertheless use the term Unknown Father, largely because of the dictates of tradition.

We next read of the "Pure Will of the Father which sends forth the Seed." This is truly the first definably masculine aspect of Deity. This Pure Will is mentioned very early on in the Mass; and in the First Hermetic Discourse we read further of the "Seed" that is the "true Good sown by the Will of God." It is associated here with the concept of Life. This may seem odd since we have previously correlated Life, or Zoe, with the feminine, as an aspect of Sophia. But when we associate the Will and the Seed with Life, we are looking at it more as a general association with the concept of life, not as the personification of Life, as represented by Zoe, Sophia's daughter. We may still see a polar dynamic here between

Light and Life, but the roles seem to be reversed; with the masculine potency of Life rising from the sea of Light. It is not uncommon to see the symbols of duality reverse their roles from time to time. This is often seen with the concepts of Spirit and Soul. The reader may consult "A Gnostic Exposition of the Three Alchemical Essentials" found in the *Clergy Handbook* for a further discussion of this.

We read next of the Holy Spirit, "Sublime Mother of the Aeons." If Sophia represents the Cosmic Womb, the Holy Spirit, Barbelo, is the Pleromic Womb. As we discussed previously, She is associated with the concept of Love, that is to say Agape, in a very technical sense as being the complement and equal to the masculine Will, or Thelema. As many are aware, Αγαπη and Θελημα each enumerate to the value of 93, to wit:

A = 1	Θ = 9
γ = 3	ε = 5
α = 1	λ = 30
π = 80	η = 8
η = 8	μ = 40
	α = 1
93	93

We will leave aside for the time being the significance of this number to point out merely that applying Greek Gematria to these words yields an equivalence. Again, we consider these to be technical terms, because they represent a formula of manifestation on all planes. Just as the *Will* sends forth the Seed, that is to say issues forth the directive, be it spiritual, astral, or physical, *Love* represents the receiving, gestating, and making manifest of that Will.

The next part of the Act of Faith concerns the Son, the Divine Child, our Lord Jesus Christ. The terms "self-generated" and "alone-begotten" are used here in place of the Greek terms autogenes and monogenes, both of which are used to describe Christ; though autogenes is certainly used more within the Gnostic texts. Christ is "self-generated" because the Logos is the very active power of God, or, as stated here, the "creative essence of the Father." Since all things have been made manifest by means of the Logos, who was, according to St. John, "in the beginning," there is no power above Him to have sent him forth. Therefore, the Logos has manifested in the world of his own volition – though not, we must add, without the cooperation of the feminine force.

The term "Author of Regeneration" was encountered first within the Mass in the First Hermetic Discourse. We are informed here that this Regeneration involves the loosening of the "bonds of matter" in order to "recall our own divine nature." This does not mean that we must reject matter or become discarnate for this regeneration and theosis to occur; but it does mean learning how to overcome the restrictions placed by the material nature upon the spirit. Once these opposite but complementary forces are understood, which may be thought of more simply as being related to the principles of expansion and contraction, they may be used harmoniously to shape and focus the subtle spiritual forces. It is this state of perfect knowledge and equilibrium that constitutes becoming "one in the fullness of God." This is true Liberty.

A final note on this aspect of the Trinity is that it will be noted that the Son is placed here as the "third person" of the Trinity, the Father being first, and the Holy Spirit, or Mother being second. This will seem somewhat foreign to many, because we have grown so accustomed to seeing the second and third positions reversed. And for the sake of linguistic familiarity we do still often say within our rituals: "Father, Son, and Holy Spirit"; for this phrase, through repeated use, has built up a massive occult power. But from a doctrinal perspective, this is the proper arrangement and sequence of the Most Holy Trinity. This is related to what we discussed previously about the Son being mistakenly attributed (largely, though not entirely, due to the *filioque*) to the feminine role, with the Holy Spirit being the product of the Union of Father and Son. (It is no wonder that the Church of Rome has the issues that it does.) Once we place the three "persons" in the proper arrangement, and with the proper gender attributions, a cohesive picture emerges of the trinitarian formula. This arrangement is, moreover, supported by the Gnostic texts themselves.

Our belief in "the communion of the Holy Saints and Prophets" is not mere rhetoric. We engage in the calling forth and communing with our venerated Masters of the Past. In this it should be noted that we hold the idea of "Saints and Prophets" in a somewhat different light than, say, the Roman Catholics. We do not have a regulated process of beatification, requiring verifiable miracles, and so on. Our Saints are those who we feel to have made some substantial contribution to the Tradition in general, or to our particular branch; it is those from whom we seek guidance even after their transition from this earthly plane. Those who would call this communication "necromancy" would not be entirely mistaken, though it bears a closer resemblance to what has been known as Spiritism. Our enlightened Brothers and Sisters – in or out of their corporeal form – are always welcome at our works.

As concerns the Transubstantiation, we believe in the real presence of Christ in the Eucharistic elements. According to our Gnostic doctrine, the Logos, which is entirely spiritual, or pneumatic, in order to manifest here below, required the assumption, first, of a psychic body, or soul, which was created by the Demiurge. This psychic Christ is the awaited messiah spoken of by the Old Testament prophets, who were, more often than not, prophets of the Demiurge rather than of the Most High. These prophecies, nevertheless, were true; and were fulfilled by the Logos wearing the psychic or astral body of Christ. This enspirited soul of the Logos/Christ was then able to incarnate in the physical, or hylic, body of Jesus. This physical envelope ceased to be relevant after the crucifixion. Whether one believes that it was simply discarded or that it was transformed into a body of Light, that is to say Spirit, and there are bases within the Gnostic Scriptures for both interpretations, the physical Jesus ceased to be a reality. The personality of Jesus, at least whatever of it belonged to the eternal, was definitively fused with the psychic body of Christ, enlivened by the Logos. So, in the transubstantiation, we are not expecting a manifestation of the physical Body and Blood of a 2,000 year old Jewish man. The Bread and Wine serve as the corporeal medium for the psychical and spiritual equivalents of "flesh" and "blood." As we mentioned earlier, the reader should consult "The Devil's Passion" in the *Clergy Handbook* for a fuller treatment of the psychic and pneumatic natures of Christ.

Our belief in "One Universal and Apostolic Church" refers to the spiritual Ecclesia, of which any earthly branch is but a temporal representation. We use the term "Universal" here instead of "Catholic" so as not to give any false impression. We could rightly use the term Catholic, but it has long lost its true meaning in the popular mindset. We do, however, claim unity with all churches that hold the succession of the apostles, which represents an ancient and unbroken initiatic chain. Whether Gnostic or orthodox, esoterically inclined or tending toward a fundamentalist literalism, there is an unseen and often unrecognized unity of sacramental efficacy among all apostolic churches.

The Act of Faith concludes with the intonation, three times, of A-U-M. Like before, this is done with the arms crossed over the chest, in the "Good Shepherd" position. Alchemically, this concludes the "Dissolution" phase, wherein, according to "Alchemy of the Eucharist," all are "brought together under a single, inseparable consciousness and belief." At this point in the liturgy, the celebrants and the congregants should be duly and truly prepared to undertake the inner work of the Mass: the High Sacramental Theurgy of the Eucharistic rite proper.

Invocation of the Holy Guardian Angel

This is an adaptation of a very powerful and traditional theurgical prayer. There is really no need to analyze this prayer, as its true significance is known by the heart alone. We shall mention, however, that while this prayer may be used by anyone to call upon the powers of the Holy Guardian Angel, those who have faithfully completed a certain ritual of High Theurgy, such as is found within the Maître Cohen section of the Christian Knights of Saint-Martin, will discover a particularly efficacious invocation here. Here, then, is this beautiful prayer pronounced by the Priest:

"O You, divine Spirit! Spirit of Wisdom, Strength, and Beauty; powerful Being of Light, with whom I desire to accomplish the most intimate union!"

"I call you! I invoke you! Come to my assistance; guide my steps on the Path of Regeneration during this whole day. Vivify me with that Divine Love that enflames you; send me continually your intellect; give me the weapons that I need in order to vanquish my spiritual enemies."

"Guide my steps toward the Truth; I abandon myself to your direction with total confidence."

"Divine Logos, that have deigned to send Your Angels to guard and guide us, help me profit from their powerful operations; help me be preserved from any fall during this day."

"Let me come to know intimately this Spirit, to which you have particularly entrusted me."

"I ask this Grace by Your Holy Blood, that has become the sigil of my reconciliation with you. Amen."

The White Phase

Offertorium

With the Offertorium begins an entirely new stage of the operation of the Mass. Alchemically, we are moving from the Black Phase, which was concerned principally with preparation and purification, into the White Phase, wherein are contained the operations of *Separation* and *Conjunction*. Both of these operations occur within the Offertorium. The process of *Separation* begins immediately. It is worthwhile to cite the "Alchemy of the Eucharist" at length concerning this operation:

The Separation is the dividing of a substance into its essential parts. In the rite of the Eucharist, this is symbolized by the priest removing the veil and paten from the Chalice at the beginning of the Offertorium, and the displaying of the water and wine cruets. At this point, the bread, wine, and water are representative of the Three Essentials: Salt, Sulphur, and Mercury respectively. It is by the proper manipulation of these three Essentials that the celebrant, who is in fact an alchemical operator, hopes to eventually "Rectify" the First Matter, that is, transform these Eucharistic elements into the Body and Blood of Christ, the Logos.

As the Priest is removing the Paten, etc., and arranging these various items, the following is recited:

"Come Thou Holy Name of Christ, Name above all names; come power from above and come highest gift; Thou Knower of the Chosen's Mysteries descend; Thou Who dost share in all noble strivers' struggles; Come! Come Thou Who givest joy to all who are at one with Thee; come and commune with us in this Eucharist which we are about to

79

make in Thy Name, in this sacrament to which we have assembled at Thy call."

Next comes an intonation of "glossolalia" – sometimes referred to as "Barbarous Names" taken from the *Pistis Sophia*. Glossolalia, or, what is sometimes known as "speaking in tongues" is a very ancient tradition in magical formula. This particular invocation from the *Pistis Sophia*, much like that found previously in the Absolution, is a mixture of simple vowel sounds, permutations of IAO, certain names, such as Sabaoth, and others familiar to the Greek Magical Papyri, and some unknown; but beyond their particular meaning (or lack thereof), it is the quality of the vibrations of sound of the intonations themselves that serve to transport the consciousness. An example of the following intonation, set to music, may be found on the ACP website (http://pleromachurch.org) as "Invocation of the Barbarous Names." Here is the invocation (for a transliteration of the Greek, see G.R.S. Mead's translation of the *Pistis Sophia*):

"Αεηιουω ιαω αωι ωια ψινωθερ θερνωψ νωψιθερ ζαγουρη παγουρη νεθμομαωθ νεψιομαωθ μαραχαχθα θωβαρραβαυ θαρναχαχαν ζοροκοθορα ιεου Σαβαωθ."

Now begins the actual offering of the Eucharistic elements, the Bread and Wine that are to be consecrated and transubstantiated into the Body and Blood of the Christ/Logos. The Priest elevates the Paten, containing the large Host, with both hands, saying:

"Blessed are You, O God, who art the Source of all things visible and invisible; the Lord of Light, Life, Love and Liberty. We offer this bread, grain of the Earth, transformed by human hands, as a token of our terrestrial nature. May it transform us and be the BODY OF CHRIST."

All respond: "Blessed be God forever," then the Paten is set down, and the Acolyte (or another assistant or the Priest) pours wine and a little water into the Chalice as the Priest says:

"Remembering the Divine and human natures of the Master Jesus, and our own Divine and human natures, we mix water with this wine, praying that we may abide in His Consciousness and He in us."

These "Divine and human natures" are the pneumatic and psychical natures spoken of previously. This corresponds directly to the alchemical *Conjunction*. Let us return to the "Alchemy of the Eucharist" to cite the relevant passage:

The Conjunction is concerned with the dynamic between Sulphur and Mercury. The Mercury is that fluid nature which is always becoming, ever changing. Sulphur represents being; that Fiery Will that imposes fixity. Sulphur and Mercury are a polar dynamic, similar to that represented in the Yin-Yang symbol of the Taoists. They also represent Spirit and Soul, and the Conjunction is often called the Sacred Marriage of Spirit and Soul. In the Eucharist, this is symbolized by the mixing of the water (Mercury) with the wine (Sulphur). The bread (Salt) will eventually become the Child of the Conjunction, *that is, the* Lapis Philosophorum, *or Philosopher's Stone, in the Red Phase.*

After the mixing of these elements in the Chalice, emblem of the alchemical crucible or athanor, and the womb of the Divine Mother, the Priest elevates the Chalice with both hands and says:

"Blessed are you O God who art the source of all things visible and invisible, the Lord of Light, Life, Love, and Liberty. We offer this wine, fruit of the Earth, transformed by human hands, as a token of our celestial nature. May it

81

transform us and be the BLOOD OF CHRIST."

     As before, all respond: "Blessed be God forever." The Priest then replace the Chalice to its central place upon the Altar. In the Mass of the ACP, the Eucharistic Bread and Wine are left entirely exposed henceforth, up to the consecration and communion proper. We are in the process of *revealing* the Mystery, not *re-veiling* it. The veil is not replaced again over the Chalice until the whole operation of the Eucharist will have been completed. A little consideration on this matter will reveal to you plainly why this is esoterically correct. I think no more need be said on this.

The Red Phase

Second Censing

The censing, here, and the following *Lavabo*, are a repetition of the purification by the four Elements found in the earlier part of the Mass. Alchemically, these purifications were found in the *Black Phase* consisting in the operations of *Calcination* and *Dissolution*. Here, we are moving from the *White Phase*, which has consisted in the *Separation* and *Conjunction*, into the *Red Phase* and its final three operations of *Fermentation, Distillation,* and *Coagulation.* But this seeming return to the *Black Phase* is, in fact, completely natural and appropriate; for the beginning of the *Ferementation* process is a sub-operation referred to as *Putrefaction,* and may be thought of as a brief and miniature *Black Phase.* These are the final purifications of the Bread and Wine, as well as of the Priest, before the Eucharistic Prayer which effects the transubstantiation.

The Priest blesses the incense, making the sign of the cross over it three times while saying, "Be thou blessed in the Name of the +Father, and of the +Son, and of the +Holy Spirit." The Altar is censed center, left, and right, three times each as before while pronouncing:

"God the Father, seen of none, God the Co-Eternal Son, and God the Holy Spirit who givest us life, pour forth Thy three-fold power in these our oblations."

The thurible is then swung in a counter-clockwise circular motion over the Eucharistic Altar and the elements it contains. This may be done as an inward-drawing spiral, while saying: "As this incense rises before Thee, O Lord, so let our prayers ascend Thy Holy Realms."

The censing is concluded by declaring: "Glory be to the Unknown Father + to the Son the Divine Logos + and to the Holy Spirit + our Celestial Mother and Consoler."

Lavabo

As the Censing was a purification of Fire and Air, so is the Lavabo that of Water and Earth, like the Asperges formerly. The Priest washes her hands in the Lavabo Font, containing Holy Water, while saying:

"O Heavenly Father, as Your rains cleanse and purify the earth, I wash my hands so that they too may be cleansed of the impurities of this world."

The Priest then continues with this Latin verse which because of its wording may seem appropriate to the *Asperges*, but which is used here because, in fact, it refers to the cleansing of oneself rather than the general purification of the Temple which is accomplished by the Asperges Rite:

"Asperges me hyssopo – et mundabor. Lavabis me aqua et super nivem dealbabor!"

This means: "Sprinkle me with hyssop, and I shall be cleansed. Wash me with water and I shall be whiter than snow."

Orate Fratres

The Latin title of this prayer means "Let us pray, brothers." Although our version of this prayer no longer opens with these words, the title has been retained, as has been done by a number of churches. Bishop Lowell Paul Wadle, in the Liturgy he composed, merely titles this portion "Exhorts the

Brethren," which is a fair and accurate description of this prayer said by the Priest:

"My Brothers and Sisters, we have built a temple for the distribution of the power of the Logos. Let us prepare these gifts as a channel for its reception. Receive, O Source of all things visible and invisible, this sacrifice of bread and wine. And may our lives be forever sanctified in Your service by the power of Christ, our Indwelling Lord. Amen."

This prayer, or "exhortation," announces the completion of the spiritual temple that has been constructed since the beginning of the Mass. It also specifically identifies the Eucharistic elements as "a channel" for the reception of the "power of the Logos." This is one of the reasons that the elements are left completely uncovered. There must be no blockage of the spiritual powers, even apparently.

Prayer Over the Gifts

The Priest prays: "May we who partake of this Holy Sacrament receive the power of Your Light and Life and be forever joined in Your Holy Wisdom." And all respond, "Amen."

The "Holy Wisdom" with which we seek to be "forever joined" is Sophia herself. On the individual scale it is the union of the Soul with the Spirit. We must first effect an inner union, an equilibrium of our fractured selves, before uniting with our celestial counterpart. This whole prayer, brief though it may be, is all about the union of the complementary forces, the Bread and Wine, the Light and Life, the Logos and Sophia. In the Union is the mystery of our Regeneration.

Prayer to the Holy Spirit

This prayer, unique even among esoteric liturgies, is dedicated wholly and exclusively to the Divine Mother. Although the feminine aspect of Deity is by no means ignored or neglected throughout our Liturgy, the references to Her are usually framed in relation to the Father and/or the Son. We often see prayers to the Father alone, as well as to Christ; but it is rare to see an expression of the feminine aspects that acknowledge Her alone, without Her value and her very existence as depending upon Her relation to the masculine aspects. Let us read this prayer, pronounced by the Priest, then take a look at some of its elements:

"O Holy Spirit, Barbelo, Divine Mother of All, may you receive us with your Glorious Embrace. Thou Who hast made Thyself known to us through your emissaries of Light and Life, of Love and Liberty; Your Aeon Sophia and her daughter Zoe, whose heavenly archetypes have been mirrored here on earth in the persons of Eve, Norea, the Virgin Mary, and Mary Magdalene; and known in the celestial realm as the Woman Clothed with the Sun; may You open our ears that we may hear Your voice of Understanding, and open our hearts that we may pour forth Thy Love."

The name Barbelo comes from several Gnostic writings, especially those commonly called "Sethian" or "Barbeloite." She is the first emanation from the One, and the second person of the Trinity. Thus, the designation of "Mother of All" is truly fitting of her, for of everything that has a beginning, She is that beginning. In the Act of Faith, She is acknowledged as the womb from which "all things are made manifest and to which they shall return." We seek, therefore, to return into that loving embrace from which we were separated in the Aeons.

The prayer then goes on to address some of the myriad

manifestations of the Divine Feminine, of which Barbelo is the archetype. First are mentioned Her "emissaries." This refers, principally, to the four Luminaries: Harmozel, Oroiael, Daveithai, and Eleleth, and also to all of the Aeons of the Pleroma that fall under these Luminaries, especially the very last Aeon, Sophia. In the great Gnostic drama, it is Sophia, the youngest daughter of Barbelo, sometimes referred to as Pistis Sophia, who made the error that was responsible for matter and the demiurge; but then worked toward her own restoration in helping to devise a plan to reclaim the part of her that was lost due to this error. When the demiurge creates Adam, it is Sophia, with the assistance of Barbelo, who sends Zoe to join with Adam and makes him live. Zoe is seen to be an aspect of Sophia, or Her daughter in some texts. In the Septuagint, Eve is called Zoe. In the Gnostic mythos, Zoe is the spiritual, enlightened aspect of the androgynous Adam. When Zoe is removed from Adam, he falls back into a state of darkness and ignorance. This is why Zoe had to return, paired with the Logos, in the person of Jesus Christ, in order to successfully effect the redemption of Adam (that is to say all of humanity).

Therefore, Eve, as the name of the human woman, is only the *image* of the true Zoe, just as the human male is not the true Adam. It is only in the reunion of these principles that the true Human emerges. But we may, nevertheless, see Eve as a *type* of Zoe, and therefore, ultimately, of Barbelo. Norea is something of a composite figure, known as the sister of Seth in certain Gnostic texts. She is treated as more of a divine being than as a mere mortal, and thus may be related more to the heavenly or pleromic Seth. In any case, she is certainly a type of the Divine Feminine, and plays a moderate role in certain Gnostic scriptures, having direct contact with the Luminary Eleleth. In the "Thought of Norea" she takes on a quite elevated role.

So much has been written on the Virgin Mary that we scarcely need to devote much space to her here. We should note, though, that the so-called orthodoxy has often attributed to her roles that are beyond her station. That is not to say that every reverence is not due to her, but to grant such titles as "Queen of Heaven" are simply not accurate from a Gnostic perspective. To be sure, no great error is committed in conflating the Mother of Christ with the Divine archetype, but in Gnosticism we embrace the multitude of feminine expressions, so we need not attribute every expression of divine femininity to one single personage. Sophia much better fits the appellation of "Queen of Heaven." As concerns iconography, though, the Holy Virgin depicted as "Queen of Heaven" may be utilized as a perfectly valid representation of Sophia.

Mary Magdalene was highly revered by the ancient Gnostics, often depicted as the most learned of the disciples of Jesus. There has been much speculation concerning the relationship between Jesus and Mary Magdalene, mainly due to the Gospel of Philip which suggests her as a sort of "companion" of Jesus. The ACP has no official doctrine concerning the nature of the personal relationship between Jesus and Mary Magdalene, as there is simply not enough historical data to draw any reasonable assumptions therefrom. But as concerns her role as an elite adept of Jesus' initiatory circle, there can be no doubt; possibly even the chief adept, or "apostle to the apostles." There are many myths and traditions surrounding the figure of Mary Magdalene, and it is probably not important that they cannot be historically verified. Gnosticism is, at its core, a religion of intuitive revelation; and it is a continual, perpetual revelation. There are a great many mysteries that may be known only through this special revelation, and the mysteries of the Magdalene and the Christos are surely such.

The image of the "Woman Clothed With the Sun" comes from John's Revelation. Most esoteric authors have equated her with either the constellation of Virgo, hence the Celestial Virgin as a counterpart to the Virgin Mary; or with the planet Venus, with its heliacal rising, thus "clothed with the sun." The author of the *Chymical Wedding of Christian Rosenkreuz* has cleverly combined these images in his initiatrix character of Virgo Lucifera. Although I personally identify this image slightly more with Venus, the character of "Virgo Lucifera" has become something of a venerated Saint for me, as the name so aptly describes this elusive being.

This short prayer to feminine Deity certainly does not give an exhaustive account of the multifold expressions of the Divine Mother, but it does acknowledge Her upon every plane of existence, without being qualified by Her male counterpart. The heresiologists, when inventing names for the various Gnostic branches, often referred to the Sethians as Barbelognostics or Barbeloites because of their special veneration for Barbelo. I would place the ACP firmly within the Barbeloite camp. We are, of course, a modern iteration of the Gnostic current; and our Christology is probably more Valentinian than strictly Sethian. But our notion of the Trinity does have a solid Sethian basis, and Barbelo, especially in the aspect of her youngest daughter, Sophia, is the true guiding force of the Church.

Eucharistic Prayer

This section represents the pinnacle of the traditional Eucharistic rite. What we have included under the title of "Eucharistic Prayer" is sometimes divided into smaller sections, such as the *Epiclesis, Institution*, etc. To return to our alchemical analysis, this section represents the *Fermentation* proper, where a true transmutation is about to take place. The Priest begins with this prayer:

"O Most High God, You are holy indeed, and all creation rightly gives You praise. All life, all holiness comes from You through Christ, our Lord, Logos of the Eternal Aeon. From age to age, You reveal Your perennial Wisdom to Your

Holy Elect, and call forth those that might partake of Your Divine Mystery."

The Priest then joins his hands together and holds them outstretched over the offerings while continuing to recite what is commonly referred to as the *Epiclesis*:

"And so, Most High God, we bring You these gifts. We ask You to make them holy by Your power to bless + to approve + and to ratify + that they may become the Body + and Blood + of Christ, the Logos."

At this, the Priest raises the bread slightly and begins the actual words of institution:

"Following the example set forth by Melchizedek, the eternal High Priest, the Master Jesus, took the bread and gave You thanks and praise. He blessed and broke the bread and gave it to His disciples, and said..."

The Priest bows slightly and reverently while pronouncing:

"Take and eat ye all of this, for THIS IS MY BODY."

The bread is now technically the Host, as it is the incorporation of the very Body of Christ. The Priest then shows the consecrated Host to the people, then places it on the Paten and genuflects in adoration. The Priest rises and continues with the words of institution:

"In like manner, when the supper was ended, he took the noble Chalice."

The Priest now raises the Chalice slightly, as previously done with the bread, saying:

"Again he gave you thanks and praise, blessed it and

gave it to His disciples, and said..."

The Priest bows slightly again and consecrates the wine thus:

"Take and drink ye all of this, for THIS IS MY BLOOD. Do this in remembrance of me."

The Priest then shows the Chalice containing the very Blood of Christ, then genuflects in adoration. The Eucharistic elements having been transubstantiated, the Priest extends her hands over them for the following prayer:

"Father, we celebrate the memory of Christ, the Eternal Logos, the repairer and our restorer of Gnosis. We, Your people and Your Priests offer unto You, O Most High God, this perfect sacrifice: the bread of Life and the cup of eternal Salvation."

"Look with favor on these offerings and accept them as once You accepted the gifts of our patriarch in the Gnosis, the bread and wine offered by Your priest Melchizedek."

"Almighty God, we pray that this sacrifice be borne to thine altar, there to be offered by Him who, as the eternal High Priest, forever offers Himself as the eternal Sacrifice."

"And as He has ordained that the heavenly sacrifice shall be mirrored here on earth through the ministry of mortals, to the end that Your holy people may be brought more closely into fellowship with You, we do pray for them who serve at this altar, that rightly celebrating the mysteries of the Most Holy Body + and Blood + of the Christ, they may be filled + with Your mighty power and blessing, O Lord of Light, Life, Love, and Liberty."

With this prayer, the sacrificial *offering* has been made, but the *sacrifice* itself is yet to come. We shall return to this notion after the Litany.

Litany

As we suggested previously, our communion with the Saints is held to be a real phenomenon. In some liturgies the litany of the Saints comes before the Eucharistic transubstantiation, but there are legitimate reasons for placing it here. While we would defend against the accusations of necromancy, there is, nevertheless, a certain relationship here to that process. As many practitioners of necromancy are well aware, images and items associated with death – performing the rite in a graveyard, utilizing bones, etc. – can help to draw the souls of the dead; and blood is considered to be the most potent attractor of all; though greatly advised against in almost every case. Now, the use of human blood attracts, for the most part (except in certain cases of offering one's blood voluntarily to draw very specific influences, or to attach oneself to some greater egregore, and some other specialized circumstances), very base, lost souls, or other lower beings or entities, even those which would be termed demonic. But the blood we have before us is not of a physical nature, but psychical and pneumatic; and the beings that it attracts are of an entirely other, higher, order. Saints, angels, and other holy beings are drawn to the blood of Christ under a similar principle as that which applies to necromancy, though on a much higher level. Even certain archons may be attracted, if they are of a disposition to assist in our work. In general, the lower beings will stay clear of an operation such as this, but even should any find themselves attracted thereto, it would only be to find some relief from their sufferings; and to the extent that they are able to receive it, none shall be denied the magnificent blessings of Christ. Does not the Sun shed its rays equally upon all?...

Because the Litany calls forth not only pure spiritual beings, but also the souls of the deceased, which may or may not have yet become wholly spiritualized (we cannot always be sure of this), this particular rite may not be considered pure theurgy, but may contain elements of what has been described as demiurgy. But such may be said for the whole Mass, since we evoke not only the pneumatic Logos, but also the psychical Christ, which serves as the envelope or "soul" for the Logos. The entire Eucharistic service, therefore, involves the Demiurge and his son, the Christ, as much as it involves the Unknown Father of Light and the Divine Child, the Logos. We shall return to this concept after our discussion of the Litany.

The Priest announces the Litany thus:

"Let us now in due and ancient fashion call upon the powers of the Most High and on all the Holy Ones who were and are and are to come, that united with them we may bravely strive for and ultimately attain to the Gnosis of Light, Life, Love, and Liberty."

At this call, all face *West*, the place of the souls of the dead, and kneel. Then begins the chanting of the Litany. The Litany is arranged as a call and response between the Priest and the two Deacons, but other clergy may participate in the response if it is desired. In our exegesis here, we will not repeat every response, but merely focus on the names invoked. We will mention, though, that the first four responses are: "Shed thy glory upon us," whereas the responses thereafter are: "Hear us and be near us."

The first four "names" are to be properly *intoned* rather than merely *chanted*. It is difficult to explain this any more clearly without an actual demonstration; which is an example of clergy formation that cannot be achieved through independent study alone, but necessitates a system of active mentorship. The first four names to be intoned are I-A-O, Sabaoth, Abraxas, and Sophia. As mentioned above, each of these names, individually, is followed by "Shed thy glory upon us," chanted by the Deacons. The name IAO is well-known from ancient Gnostic and pre-Gnostic usage. Its usage by the ACP is primarily for its unique vibratory qualities. It is also given in certain Gnostic texts as the name of one of the archons created by the demiurge. But this does not make it "evil." The archons are not demons, *per se*. For the most part they show no will of their own outside of what is imposed upon them. The "evil" that they do is merely the carrying out of a directive. Recall too that the 72 disciples, upon returning to Jesus, declared that even the demons submitted to them in His Name. In any case, the use of IAO here is less in the archontic sense than merely to the activation of energy centers. But if the archon of this name is invoked thereby, it is only in the service of, and to the glory of the Most High.

Sabaoth comes from the Hebrew meaning "Lord of hosts." In Gnostic literature, Sabaoth is another of the archons created by the demiurge. In an astounding feat of will and righteous rebellion, Sabaoth recognizes the supremacy of Sophia, worships her, and is elevated in station by her. Not having its origin in the Pleroma, Sabaoth does not ascend that high, but he is raised unto the very heights of the psychical realm, where he assists Sophia and the Logos in their cosmic mission. Could an archon, by aligning itself with spiritual works, be eventually spiritualized itself? It is a question worth considering.

Abraxas, sometimes spelled as Abrasax, appears in a number of Gnostic writings and contexts. The role of Abraxas seems to be of a higher, Aeonic sort; but there also seems to be a solar representation, as the Greek letters which compose the name add up to 365, to wit:

$$A = 1$$
$$\beta = 2$$
$$\rho = 100$$
$$\alpha = 1$$
$$\xi = 60$$
$$\alpha = 1$$
$$\varsigma = 200$$
$$\overline{}$$
$$365$$

Abraxas is often attributed to the system of Basilides, but was likely in use in various Greco-Egyptian magical practices even earlier. The image of Abraxas, often depicted as a composite being, with a human trunk and arms, a rooster's head, and serpents for legs, is found upon many Gnostic amulets known as "gems." Abraxas is invoked here both because of the vibratory quality of the name, and because of the long tradition of associating Abraxas with the protection of the Gnostics.

Sophia needs no further explanation here. She is included in these invocations because these are all beings that are known to work directly within the cosmos, either because they are cosmic (i.e. psychical) in nature and origin, such as Sabaoth, or that this realm is simply the plane of activity upon which they are destined to work. Sophia, though She has her origin in the Pleroma, and is herself an Aeon of the Pleroma, nevertheless resides outside of the Pleroma until her final restoration. She is not necessarily enmeshed in the Cosmos, for tradition states that she is in a position that is in the veil that divides what is below from what is above. But as such, she has a direct influence over the activities of the sub-Pleromic realms. It is not that she interferes directly, as does the demiurge, but she is an ever-present subtle influence, and readily accessible to her followers.

95

The next part of the Litany calls out to "All the souls of the Holy Gnostics during the Aeons." In this, we may take the word "aeon" as both an indefinitely long period of time, and also in the sense of those Holy Souls who have ascended into the Aeonic realms. The response to this is "Hear us and be near us," which is then the response for all the following names. The organization of the following names is thus: 1st, the Apostles most closely associated with the Gnostic tradition; 2nd, the early Gnostic teachers, whom we might call the Gnostic Doctors of the Church; 3rd, the Gnostic-inspired teachers of the middles ages; and lastly the great mystics and bishops whose doctrines would lay the foundation for the modern Gnostic Church, up to the present. The list is not comprehensive, and it may be lengthened or shortened according to the desire of the celebrants.

Mary Magdalene is the first name listed among the Apostles. The ACP recognizes her supremacy among the Apostles, and acknowledges her as "Apostle to the Apostles." For this she is given preeminence of place among all the souls of the deceased whom we call forth as witnesses to our work.

John the Baptist is unique within our tradition as being not a disciple of Jesus, but as an *initiator* of Jesus. It was the baptism of Jesus at the hands of John that inaugurated the ministry of Jesus on earth. There are some traditions that place Jesus and John the Baptist within the same secret order of mystics, wherein John was the senior; a circle which may have later included Dositheus and Simon Magus.

The Apostle John is held in a very high regard by the Gnostics. The canonical Fourth Gospel, ascribed to John, is believed by many to contain Gnostic or proto-Gnostic elements, especially within the prologue. The commentary on this Gospel by the Valentinian Heracleon is considered to be one of the very earliest examples of New Testament exegesis. The Cathars held this Gospel in especially high regard and used it ritually. And it is found upon the altars, not only of Freemasonry, but of many an esoteric and occult order. John's

Apocalypse or *Revelation* is also held to be of an extreme mystical significance. There are many mystical exegeses on this work, and it is used ritually by many occult bodies. Certain alchemists have seen therein a depiction of the various phases and operations of the alchemical process. See our "Liturgy of Saint John the Divine" also called the "Mass of the Seven Seals" (at http://pleromachurch.org) for an introduction to this alchemical interpretation. And of course the non-canonical Johannine literature, such as the *Acts of John* and the explicitly Gnostic *Apocryphon of John* have found great praise within Gnostic circles.

The Apostle Thomas is included here because of his important role in the Gnostic tradition. In addition to the importance among the Gnostics of works such as the *Gospel of Thomas*, Thomas himself figures among the Gnostic texts as one who is highly enlightened, and who recognized the knowledge and wisdom of Mary Magdalene.

The Apostle Philip does not receive much attention among the canonical texts; but the Valentinian *Gospel of Philip* is attributed to him, we may assume, not without cause. He may also have been associated with Simon Magus.

Simon Magus is often considered to be the first Gnostic. While he is generally considered to be an actual historical personage, there are so many legends and traditions surrounding this first century Samaritan Gnostic, that it is difficult to sort out the kernels of fact. His doctrine seems to have included many proto-elements of the Gnostic mythos that would be elaborated further by later teachers.

Dositheus was another early Gnostic teacher, contemporary with Simon Magus, and likely from the same mystical or theological school, which tradition places under the leadership of John the Baptist.

Menander was another first-century Samaritan Gnostic, very likely a disciple of Simon Magus, who went on to teach at Antioch. His doctrine shares many similarities with that of Simon Magus, but does not yet represent the fully fleshed-out Gnostic doctrine of the second century.

Saturninus, or Satornilos, is believed to have been a disciple of Menander. His doctrine is even more developed, beginning to look much closer to the Gnostic notions of the demiurge, etc.

Basilides was a second-century Gnostic teacher. Not much survives of his work except second-hand, through the heresiologists, but his doctrine has a number of similarities with the Sethian and Valentinian schools, including a doctrine of Sophia and the demiurge.

Valentinus is one of the most well-known and respected of the ancient Gnostic teachers. Born in Egypt around the turn of the first century, he is said to have received his spiritual tradition from a disciple of Paul named Theudas. The system of Valentinus, while sharing many similarities with the Sethian and even Basilidean systems, was particularly ingenious in how it sought to reconcile the Gnostic and "orthodox" theologies and practices. Valentinus integrated so well into "Catholic" Christianity, that it is reported by Tertullian that he was nearly elected bishop of Rome. The Valentinians were one of the most wide-spread and successful of the ancient Gnostic sects.

Bardaisan, or Bardesanes, was a late second/early third-century Gnostic from Syria. He is known more by reputation than through his actual works, of which none, unfortunately, remain. He is typically associated with the Valentinian and/or Thomasine school.

Clement of Alexandria is a rather difficult character to discern. He was not Gnostic in the classical sense, although he did appropriate the term, and sought gnosis as a means of salvation. He was critical of the Gnostics, but adopted not a few of their concepts. Although he does not fall strictly within the category of the Gnostic Doctors, we nevertheless revere him for his contributions to the mystical Christian gnosis.

Origen, like Clement, came up through the same Catechetical School of Alexandria. Though he was no friend of the classical Gnostics, he, like Clement before him, appropriated certain Gnostic concepts, and advocated for an allegorical exegesis of the Scriptures. The teachings of Origen – who would later be declared a heretic by the orthodoxy – have been largely adopted by many within the esoteric Christian community. One notable example is the doctrine taught by the mystical priest-healer Abbé Julio. Robert Ambelain, in his biography of Abbé Julio, makes this case convincingly. Ambelain himself adopted the theology of Origen as that of his Eglise Gnostique Apostolique. The ACP preserves some of the Origenian doctrines, such as the notion of universal redemption, but in general our Gnosticism is much more aligned with the primitive Gnostics; a position that the original Eglise Gnostique was tending towards, but from which its later permutations would gradually move away. But as with Clement of Alexandria, we feel that Origen's contributions to the Christian mystical doctrine are worthy of veneration.

Hypatia, daughter of the noted Alexandrian mathematician Theon, was not technically a Gnostic, but rather a Neoplatonic philosopher. Because of the close association modern Gnostics hold with Neoplatonism, Hypatia is a greatly honored figure. She was brutally tortured and murdered by orthodox Christian zealots. She is thus considered by us as a Holy Martyr.

Esclarmonde de Foix, sister of the Comte de Foix, was a Cathar Parfaite (Perfect) who is known for having confronted "St." Dominic of the infamous Inquisition. Some legends attributed great heroic and even supernatural feats to her. The Cathars in general, and their close cousins the Bogomils, are generally thought of as a French phenomenon, but were in fact spread throughout many parts of Europe, especially in the east and south. The Cathars, like the Bogomils and the Paulicans, were strictly dualistic, equating the creator of this world with Satan, which is a position more extreme than the Gnostic doctrine of the demiurge, but which has undoubtedly descended from it. Despite their somewhat extreme views, the Cathars were tolerant and peace-loving, and their moral reputation was beyond reproach. The Cathars were persecuted cruelly by the Roman Catholic Church, culminating in the Albigensian Crusade which killed literally hundreds of thousands. One of the last Cathar strongholds was at Montségur, where hundreds burned to death for refusing to renounce their faith. Esclarmode de Foix was among them.

Joachim of Fiore was a 12th century mystical monastic who taught a doctrine similar to certain ancient Gnostic concepts of dividing history into three periods or "Ages": the Age of the Father, which corresponds to the era of the Old Testament; the Age of the Son, corresponding to the period since the birth of Christ; and the Age of the Holy Spirit, which he anticipated to begin in the year 1260. Leaving aside the specific date of 1260 or of other inaugural dates, the idea of three distinct ages of humanity has recurred frequently among Gnostic and esoteric movements. The final Age of Joachim, that of the Holy Spirit, indicates a time when humanity will be in direct communication with the Holy Spirit, without the need for a mediator.

The Knights Templar were a monastic military order founded in 1118 or 1119 with the mission to protect pilgrims traveling to the Holy Land. Tradition holds that while in the East, the Templars encountered a number of mystical sects into which some of them may have been initiated, and whose doctrine and rituals may have been incorporated into the Order to some extent. In the early 14th century, Pope Clement V and the king of France, Phillippe-le-Bel, or Philip the Fair (Philip IV) plotted to destroy the Templar Order in order to seize their lands and wealth, which indeed was done when an arrest decree was executed throughout Europe (though especially in France) against all Templars simultaneously on Friday, October 13, 1304. Jacques de Molay of Burgundy, the last Grand Master of the Templars, was burnt alive as a heretic in 1314. It is reported that upon his funeral pyre he called to

God to bring justice to the treacherous pope and king within the year; and within a year they would both, indeed, meet their final justice. There are legends and traditions of successions of Grand Masters after de Molay, but these should not be taken literally. The successions must be seen as an allegory, at best, of the tradition of spiritual chivalry which has long permeated the modern Gnostic and mystical Christian tradition. But the Templar successions and traditions which are found today among the esoteric orders, churches, and societies, while perhaps not having a direct lineal succession from the last Grand Master, are still important in their own right. And the blood of the Templar martyrs certainly enlivens the egregore of modern Templarism.

Martinès de Pasqually is the father, or perhaps grand-father, of the Martinist tradition. Pasqually was the founder of a branch of occult Masonry called the Knight Masons Elus Coëns of the Universe. The Elus Coëns, or Elus Cohen as it is more commonly rendered in modern times, was an order of High Theurgy whose object was to effect the regeneration and reintegration of its initiates into their original spiritual rights and privileges. The doctrine of Martinès is layed out in allegorical form in his *Treatise on the Reintegration of Beings*, which has been called by some a biblical exegesis. But this is not quite a proper description. What it truly represents is a complete esoteric doctrine veiled in biblical allegory. For example, one would not look at the Masonic allegory of Hiram Abiff and describe it as a biblical exegesis. Pasqually's *Reintegration* must be viewed in the same light, and in so doing, one will cut more easily into the heart of his doctrine.

Louis-Claude de Saint-Martin was one of the most well-known of Pasqually's disciples. Known as *le Philosophe Inconnu* or the Unknown Philosopher, he was a prolific author on mystical subjects. Internalizing the operative works of the Elus Cohen, he sought a more purely mystical "Way of the Heart." His disciples were initiated not through any Masonic-like formulaic ritual, but by a simple laying-on of hands and a general instruction in the principles of spiritual reintegration. The works of Jacob Bœhme, some of which Saint-Martin translated into French, became as a second master to him. But although his personal ideology drifted somewhat from that of Pasquallys, he never renounced or spoke ill of his old teacher and school. The teachings of Saint-Martin would greatly influence the mystical and occult thought of the 19th century and up to the present day.

Jean-Baptiste Willermoz was another influential disciple of Pasqually. Though perhaps not as well-known as Saint-Martin, his influence upon the esoteric world has been great. While Saint-Martin moved away from the Masonic structures, Willermoz, a long time active Freemason, brought Pasqually's teachings even closer to the Masonic Fraternity, by effectively transforming the French branch of German Templar Masonry, known as the *Strict Observance*, into the body of spiritual chivalry that would serve as a portal to the inner teachings of the Elus Cohen. Thus was born the Chevaliers Bienfaisants de la Cité Sainte, or Knights Beneficent of the Holy City. Willermoz's rectified Scottish Masonry would eventually lose much of its mystical character, that is until it was revivified decades later by inheritors of the modern Gnostic tradition such as Robert Ambelain, of whom we shall soon speak.

Bernard Raymond Fabré-Palaprat founded a "restored" Ordre du Temple, as well as an esoteric Johannite Church of Primitive Christians. Having been consecrated a bishop in 1810 by Guillaume Mauviel into the apostolic lineage of Scipione Cardinal *Rebiba*, he founded the Johannite Church between 1828 and 1830 upon the principles of a redacted version of the *Gospel of John* and its commentary, the Levitikon. While the Johannite Church would itself be rather short-lived, its episcopal lineage would be incorporated later into the Gnostic Church.

Marie, Countess of Caithness and Duchess of Pomar, was very influential in the European occult milieu of the latter

19th century. She was a friend of Madame Blavatsky and one of the earliest members of the Theosophical Society. She was linked to nearly every major occult movement of the day, including Martinism and the Hermetic Order of the Golden Dawn, if not as a member, certainly through her personal acquaintance and influence upon their members and leadership. And it was within her Spiritist oratory that Jules Doinel would receive his visions instructing him to reestablish the Gnostic Church.

Tau Valentin II was the episcopal nomen of Jules-Benoît Stanislas Doinel du Val-Michel. Doinel received a series of visions and communications from deceased Cathar Bishops, from Sophia-Acamôth, and from the very Aeon Christ. It was through these Spiritist communications that he was spiritually consecrated and instructed to establish the Gnostic Church, which was carried out in 1890, which year he declared to be the beginning of the "Era of the Gnosis Restored." It is from Doinel's Gnostic Church that nearly all modern Gnostic Churches have derived; and the adoption of the prefix of Tau, that is to say the tau cross "T" has been adopted almost universally by Gnostic Bishops.

Mar Timotheos was the episcopal nomen of Joseph-René Vilatte, a bishop in the Antiochian-Jacobite succession. Vilatte is well known throughout the Independent Catholic movement, and the history of his activities and of the churches that have descended from him are well documented in works such as Peter Anson's *Bishops at Large*. Vilatte was active in both France and the United States, especially in Wisconsin. His apostolic lineage would be incorporated into one of the major branches of the Gnostic Church, and is considered as one of the primary successions within the ACP (see "Successio Apostolica" in the *Clergy Handbook* or at the ACP website). His Eglise Catholique Française was inherited by the famous French priest-healer Abbé Julio, of whom we shall speak shortly.

Jean Sempé was a faith healer about whom little is

known except what has been related by his chief disciple and successor Abbé Julio. He was regarded by Abbé Julio as a wise and pious man who had received the spiritual gift of healing, and who was able to pass this gift to others.

Julien-Ernest Houssay, or Abbé Julio, had been a Roman Catholic priest who was strong-armed out, not because of his mystical inclinations, but because he dared to expose the licentiousness of the Catholic clergymen of the day. Abbé Julio was known for his miraculous powers of healing and was beloved by his parishioners and members of the community. After leaving the Church of Rome, Houssay was consecrated as a bishop under the direction of Villatte by Paolo Miralglia Gulatti. Abbé Julio was friends with and a mentor to the successor of Doinel, Léonce-Eugène Joseph Fabre des Essarts, known in ecclesia as Tau Synésius. In fact, he maintained close relations with several within the Gnostic and esoteric community. His magnum opus was a work published in three volumes, the translations of which we have made and are published by Triad Press as *Grand Marvelous Secrets, Liturgical Prayers,* and the *Secret Book of Grand Exorcisms and Benedictions.* A detailed account of the fascinating life of Abbé Julio may be found in the work by Robert Ambelain, also translated by us, *Abbé Julio: His Life, His Work, His Doctrine.*

Tau Vincent is the episcopal nomen of the eminent Dr. Gérard Encausse, better known as Papus. Papus was at the very center of French occultism at the fin-de-siècle. There is no more prolific author of the period on occult subjects, and Papus' knowledge extended to nearly every branch. He was a principal promulgator of the Martinist doctrine, and one of the first bishops consecrated by Doinel into the Gnostic Church. He ultimately broke from the original Gnostic Church to join with Jean Bricaud and others in the schismatic Eglise Catholique Gnostique. This latter branch, however, would long outlast its parent, and become a primary source for a multitude of Gnostic Churches. Papus' contributions to the modern Gnostic and occult tradition cannot be overstated. He was a true conduit for the Inititic Tradition. At the time of his death in 1916 – brought about by the tuberculosis that he had contracted as an army doctor on the front lines in the First World War – he was not only Grand Master of the Martinist Order that he had helped to found, but also head of the Ordre Kabbalistique de la Rose+Croix, and Grand Hierophant of the Rite Ancien et Primitif de Memphis-Misraim.

Tau Jean II was the episcopal nomen of Jean Bricaud. Originally a bishop of the Eglise Gnostique under Tau Synésius, Bricaud, a Martinist S:::I::: left the Church along with Papus and others after a new constitution was drafted, in 1906, which no longer connected the Gnostic Church to Martinism, as it had been nearly since inception. A new body was formed, one that Tau Synésius called "a schism and a heresy." This church, originally called Eglise Catholique Gnostique, changed its name shortly after to Eglise Gnostique Universelle, or Universal Gnostic Church. Bricaud was elected Patriarch of this church, and some years after its foundation, he received an additional episcopal consecration by Louis-Marie-François Giraud, who had been consecrated by Abbé Julio into the "Vilatte" succession. Although he received a certain amount of criticism in his day, bishop Bricaud nevertheless deserves our veneration as an important link in the *initiatic chain.*

Tau Harmonius was the episcopal nomen of Constant Chevillon, who succeeded Bricaud as Patriarch of the EGU. Chevillon was a true martyr of the Gnosis. He worked tirelessly toward the furtherance of the modern Gnostic tradition in the harshest of environments of Nazi-occupied France. Chevillon was assassinated in cold blood by the Vichy régime on March 23, 1944. He may have had his life and work cut short, but he was none-the-less another vital link in the initiatic and apostolic line of succession that has descended to us in our day. And the blood of martyrs *always* serves to strengthen the egregore of a movement.

Tau Jean III is the episcopal nomen of the late Patriarch of the Gnosis, Robert Ambelain. Few have done as much as he to develop and propagate the Gnostic and occult current unto the present day. As an associate of Constant Chevillon, Georges de Lagrèze, and so many other Gnostic and occult luminaries, he was one of the principal founders of the 1943 reconstruction of the Order of Elus-Cohen. He was consecrated a bishop in 1946 by Roger Ménard under Patriarch Victor Blanchard (Tau Targelius) in a church whose name was, confusingly, identical to that of Chevillon (this is due to a former schism). Upon the death of bishop Blanchard in 1953, Ambelain founded his own branch as the Eglise Gnostique Apostolique. Some years later, bishop Charles-Henri Dupont, successor to Chevillon's EGU, authorized Ambelain to fuse the Patriarchate of the EGU with that of the EGA, with Ambelain as Patriarch. This fusion was known variously as the Eglise Gnostique Apostolique Universelle, Eglise Gnostique Catholique Apostolique, and other similar designations in French, Latin, Spanish, and Portuguese. Ambleain, perhaps more than any other personage of the modern era, is responsible for bringing to us not only the Gnostic and apostolic lines of succession, but also those of Martinism, the Elus-Cohen, the OKR+C, the Rose+Croix d'Orient, the Ancient and Primitive Rite of Memphis-Misraim, and others. He also authored several indispensable books and articles on esoteric doctrine and history. It is after this great and Venerable Master that the Mother-Parish of the ACP has been named.

Tau Ogdoad Orfeo I is the episcopal nomen of the mysterious Haitian adept Lucien-François Jean-Maine. L-F Jean-Maine, after receiving initiation into the Voodoo traditions of his native Haiti, as well as into the bodies that had descended from the Cohen Temples established there by Pasqually himself, traveled to Europe where he studied with adepts and followers of the American Rosicrucian, Paschal Beverly Randolph, including, possibly, Maria Naglowska.

106

Litany

Jean-Maine seems to have been involved too with the Memphis-Misraim bodies of Spain, as well as with the Gnostics there, where he received the episcopal consecration. He is said to have met with Papus in around 1910 to exchange consecrations and initiatic lineages. Upon his return to Haiti, Jean-Maine perpetuated these lines of succession through various esoteric bodies, such as the Ecclesia Gnostica Spiritualis and La Couleuvre Noire.

Tau Ogdoad Orfeo III was the episcopal nomen of Jean-Maine's son, Hector-François Jean-Maine. Hector-François received episcopal consecration at the hands of his father, along with Robert Ambelain, in 1953, thus uniting several important ecclesiastical lines of succession. H-F Jean-Maine was the principal consecrator of His Beatitude Michael-Paul Bertiaux in 1963, in Haiti. Bertiaux inherited the entire Jean-Maine system upon the death of H-F Jean-Maine in 1984. The primary apostolic succession of the ACP comes through the line descending from bishop Bertiaux, who has been most supportive and encouraging of our mission.

Tau Charles was the episcopal nomen of bishop Roger St. Victor-Herard. Bishop Herard was the Primate for North America of the EGCA. During his tenure, the Patriarchate of the EGCA was dissolved, making the North American Primacy an independent jurisdiction. Bishop Herard's appointed successor left the Church, but one other Primate was created: bishop Jorge Enrique Rodiguez-Villa.

Tau Johannes XIII was the episcopal nomen of the aforementioned bishop Jorge Rodriguez. Rodriguez's ministry was primarily directed towards the Spanish-speaking population; but as the only remaining Primate in Herard's succession, it fell upon him to fill the vacant seat of the North American Primacy, which he did in 2000 by appointing bishop Valdiveso Matthews to that office.

Tau Iohannes Harmonius was the episcopal nomen of bishop John Cole of the EGCA. Bishop Cole is not within our direct episcopal lineage, but his kindness, humility, and

107

tireless efforts in service to the Light of Gnosis were commendable. He was the first Grand Master of the Ancient Martinist Order and an initiate of the Ancient and Primitive Rite of Memphis-Misraim, among other associations. Bishop Cole will always be remembered by us for his fraternal spirit. The Litany concludes with the Priest chanting: "All the Apostles, Prophets, Bishops, Priests, & Martyrs of the Gnosis." To which all respond: "Hear us and be near us, now and forever." This helps to address the multitudes of luminous individuals whom we have, unfortunately had to omit due to the constraints of space and time. The celebrants, however, are free to adapt this Litany to their own needs and inclinations. If enough time is available, the Litany may be increased to almost any desired length. There are so many worthy lights of our tradition that the present list could be easily tripled or quadrupled and still barely scratch the surface. Some will notice even in the list that we have just given an augmentation from that which appears in the *Lectionary* and the *Clergy Handbook*. Likewise, if there are time constraints, the Litany may be pared back to include only the initial invocations, perhaps with the Apostles and some of the Gnostic Doctors. The Litany is flexible in this way, but it should not be discarded altogether. It is a very potent rite, and when we call out, "Hear us and be near us," it is a very real appeal to the actual presence of these discarnate beings. These holy Masters of the Past can and will heed this call, and their presence can become a palpable manifestation. I have personally witnessed the hazy apparitions of the Passed Masters at their call. While initially jarring, their appearance is never disturbing or disruptive. They come simply to participate in the celebration of the most holy sacrament, just like the rest of us.

Kyrie

The "Kyrie" is a sung call and response, wherein the Priest chants "Kyrie Eleison," and all others repeat it in imitation of the Priest. The same then occurs for the words "Christe Eleison." Then the Priest along with everyone else sings "Kyrie Eleison" a final time all together. These words mean: Lord have mercy. Christ have mercy.

The Priest then prays, "Welcome into Your kingdom, O Lord, our departed brothers and sisters in the Gnosis." Then he recites:

"Mother and Father united as one;
Wisdom and Strength through Your eternal Son;
We are divided for Love's sake;
That through our union we may make
Ourselves as symbols of Heaven on Earth;
In life, in death, and in rebirth!"

The Priest then concludes this section with this petition: "Oh Christ our Lord who gives us all these gifts, bless them and made them holy."

Pater Noster

The Pater Noster (Latin for "Our Father") is also called the Lord's Prayer because it was pronounced by Jesus himself to God the Father. This prayer is not only beautiful, but deeply impactful and esoterically rich. The best exegeses on the Pater are the "Meditations on the 'Pater'" and the "Esotericism of the Pater Noster," both by Papus, and both translated by us and posted on the ACP website. There is really nothing original that we may add to these excellent pieces, so let us just give the text of the prayer. The Priest announces the prayer: "Let us pray with confidence in the words the Master Jesus gave us." Then everybody together recites:

"Our Father who art in Heaven, hallowed be Thy Name;
Thy kingdom come, Thy will be done,
On Earth as it is in Heaven.
Give us this day, our daily bread,
And forgive us our debts, as we have also forgiven our debtors.
And leave us not in temptation, but deliver us from evil,
For Thine is the Kingdom, and the Power, and the Glory, forever and ever. Amen."

In conclusion, the Priest stretches out her hands, praying: "Deliver us Lord from the evil of ignorance, and grant us peace, love, and light in our day."

Breaking of the Bread

We mentioned earlier that the Body and Blood of Christ had been offered, but that the actual Sacrifice had not yet taken place. The fractioning of the bread is precisely that Sacrifice. Now, the bread is Host to both the pneumatic Logos as well as the psychic Christ. The Logos, which is pure spirit, is inseparable and impervious to any operation upon it. It is therefore the psychic body of Christ that is being sacrificed here. And we must not beat around the bush, it is to the Demiurge himself, the god of Moses and father of the psychic Christ, that this sacrifice is made. For, the Most High God requires no such human sacrifice. The only sacrifice suitable to the All, the Absolute, is the "reasonable sacrifice" mentioned in the Second Hermetic Discourse; that is to say the sacrifice born of the mind. This human sacrifice, carried out over and over unto the ages, is none other than the one demanded by the god of the Old Testament, who previously demanded the blood of animals upon his altars, but finally was sated by the sacrifice of his only son; sacrificed in perpetuity. This rite, therefore, or at least this portion, is in fact a rite of demiurgy, or High Demiurgy, if there be such a thing. This sacrifice may be seen as a sort of second separation; but unlike the first, wherein the constituent base elements were separated in order to be re-formed perfectly, it is the separation of the Spirit (Logos) from the Soul (Christ), so that the Logos may reascend to the Pleroma and the psychical Christ may sit at the right hand of his father in the astral realm. Alchemically, this is similar to the Distillation, wherein the pure "spirit" is released.

Herein is the mystery of the New Covenant. The various Covenants depicted in the Old Testament have all been with the Demiurge; and the New Covenant is likewise. The Most High does not demand a "Contract" with us. Contracts are made between parties who each have a mutual benefit to gain. The Most High God can receive nothing, because it is the *very source* of all. Therefore, there cannot be any contract or "Covenant" between the Most High God and any other being, for all is given freely. The New Covenant, or contract, therefore, stipulates that regular animal sacrifices will no longer be exacted, and that a certain amount of grace will be offered in exchange for the sacrifice of his son, which is to be repeated in perpetuity in lieu of the animals, which did not serve to sate his anger and bloodlust. Through the mediation of the psychic Christ, we are spared from the very worst of the wrath of his father. In fact, the old law has been utterly annuled in favor of the law of Love. This was possible only because it was the Logos, united with Zoe, who put on the psychic Christ to act on our behalf.

Let us begin to look at the Priest's words:

"O Divine Light, You show Yourself this day upon countless altars and yet are one and indivisible. In token of Thy great Sacrifice, we rend...this, Thy Holy Body, that we may be as Thou art."

When we pray to Christ of "Thy great Sacrifice" it is really the sacrifice of having incarnated into this lower world that we are referring to. And in rending the body, we are releasing that spiritual essence that it may be reunited in the Pleroma, which is indeed the state that we seek for ourselves. At the words "we rend..." the Priest breaks the Host in half. Just as the Host is the real Body of Christ, so too is its rending a real sacrificial act. The ceremony of the Mass, even of this sacrificial act, is couched in terms of Love and Light; and this is not in error. But one should also bear in mind and feel deeply the solemnity and sorrow for the violent act that we must commit against so pure a being for the sake of humanity. To full internalize the significance of this is to realize, truly, what it means to be a Priest. Let us continue...

"Through this ancient and sacred tradition, all Heaven

and Earth are united in Thy Consciousness, Thy Love, and Thy Will. And as the One became many, only to restore all to the Pleroma, so too, in the breaking of this bread, we are one with Thee, as Thou art one with the Father."

At this, the Priest breaks off a small piece from the bottom of the left side of the broken Host – emblematic, on one level, of the wound inflicted to the left side of Jesus as he hung upon the cross – and with it makes the sign of the cross over the Chalice, touching it at each of the cardinal points, then drops the piece into the Chalice. The Priest then forms the shape of a triangle with this thumbs and forefingers over the Chalice, and blows through this triangle upon the surface of the Blood, three crosses of air. After this, the Priest intones:

"Through Him and with Him, and in Him;
In the Unity of the Holy Spirit;
All glory and honor are Yours Almighty Father,
Forever and ever."

Then all intone together: "Amen."

This section is concluded with the following prayer of the Priest:

"Let us pray. Adoration be to Thee, O Most High God, Father of all Fatherhood, and to Thee, O Mother of all, who in the incarnation of Your Logos have mystically provided us with the Sacrament of His Body and Blood, that by partaking of this Mystery, we may reunite within ourselves the fragments of Your Divinity dispersed throughout the Cosmos. Holy, Holy, Holy, are You, the Father and Mother of the Treasury of the Light, now and unto the countless ages. Amen."

In the above prayer, at the words "Holy, Holy, Holy," the Priest should make his right hand into a fist and strike his breastbone at each "Holy"; not too hard, but firmly enough to

113

feel a good thump. There is a therapeutic practice called the "thalamus thump" to which this practice is related. It therefore has not only a symbolic value, but an actual physical benefit as well.

Theurgic Consecration

In this rite, we return to the Pentagrammaton, the notion of which was introduced in the Preliminary Rites, and expounded upon in our discussion of the First Hermetic Discourse. In Qabalistis lore, the Hebrew alphabet is considered to have originated in the divine realm. That is to say that there is a divine archetype attached to each of the characters which serve as their earthly representation. So, when we operate "by the virtue of" such or such letter, it is the divine archetype that we are drawing upon and connecting to our work. In so doing, and especially considering that this rite is structured around the very highest and holiest of divine names, it is a true rite of theurgy in the most literal sense.

This operation has been considered by some to be controversial, principally because it is an operation that is being performed upon the consecrated Body and Blood. Additionally, it involves a counter-clockwise circum-ambulation of the Altar which has been associated by some, albeit wholly erroneously, with evil or black magical practices. Far from being an act of desecration, the culmination of this rite reenacts the very process of the reparation of the Pleroma, and the full spiritualization of the Eucharistic elements. Concerning the counter-clockwise motion, the reason is two-fold. First, there is the following of the four letters of the Tetragrammaton which, of course, in the Hebrew, are written from right to left. Secondly, as mentioned in the section concerning the Second Hermetic Discourse, the counter-clockwise motion tends to draw in; and in this ceremony very powerful forces are being drawn down to the focal point of our operation.

The Priest begins by taking up the Dagger and facing

East. While pronouncing the following, she draws the letter YOD in the air with the Dagger and intones the name, thus:

"By the virtue of ' I call forth the power of IAO to join in this Holy Sacrifice."

After the drawing of the letter, the arms are outstretched while reciting the rest. Then the arms are brought down in a manner that the hands are together before the Priest, Dagger between them pointed up. The Priest bows her head a little in reverence and walks 270° counter-clockwise, that is to say from the East, through the North and West, stopping at the South. Here, a similar action is performed, with the drawing of the letter and intonation of the Name:

"By the virtue of ה I call forth the power of SABAOTH to join in this Holy Sacrifice."

The Priest lowers the arms as before, and walks in the same manner another 270° counter-clockwise, through the East and North, stopping in the West. The actions are preformed thus:

"By the virtue of ו I call forth the power of ABRAXAS to join in this Holy Sacrifice."

The same procession is made again, walking counter-clockwise to the North, and again:

"By the virtue of ה I call forth the power of SOPHIA to join in this Holy Sacrifice."

After this, the priest travels 270° counter-clockwise once more, making the third complete circuit, to return to the East. Here, the Priest faces the Eucharistic Altar, Dagger in hand with arms outstretched, drawing the letter in the air at the appropriate place:

"The Son would not be the Father without wearing the Father's Name. So by the Power of the Holy Tetragrammaton, and by virtue of the Tri-Unity of the Holy Letter ש, I call forth the power of the Author of Regeneration, the Repairer of Souls, the Destroyer of Death..."

At this point, the Priest begins slowly lowering the Dagger into the Chalice while intoning the Name, and the Dagger is held in place for the remaining recitation:

"יהשוה to pour forth Thy powers into this Holy Sacrifice and transmute these elements of bread and wine into the Divine Body and Blood of the Logos."

The Priest then makes three crosses with the Dagger in the Chalice. Notice that in the above language it mentions specifically the "*Divine* Body and Blood of the *Logos*." This is to indicate that there is nothing left of the psychical that we are dealing with. For, although the psychical sacrifice was necessary to maintain the agreement set forth with the Demiurge via the New Covenant, it is only the pure spiritual power of the Logos that will work toward the spiritualization of our own soul. Thus, by the end of the Theurgic Consecration, the Distillation has completed, and we see the Coagulation of the true Philosopher's Stone, as related by Robert Ambelain in *Spiritual Alchemy:*

And it is here we find the true Philosophical Stone of Spiritual Alchemy: *the Eucharist, in which* Water, *image of the Mercury of the Wise and of the Church, is united in the Chalice, image of the crucible, with* Wine, *symbol of the Sulphur of the Wise and Christ. Moreover, from this union of the Philosophical Sun (the Wine) and the Philosophical Moon (the Water), of these newlyweds called the* "Red Bridegroom"

116

and the "White Bride," *according to the treatise by Ripley, join together as the Philosophical Earth (the Corn), symbol of the Salt of the Wise. It is the fusion of these three terms which then constitute the Spiritual Chrysopage, by which man is identified with God, as Lead becomes Gold in the heart of the Matras.*

Communion

The Priest then elevates the Body and Blood, proclaiming:

"Behold the Divine Light which lighteth every man that cometh into the world. May the communion of these Holy Mysteries be to the regeneration of both soul and body. Let us draw nigh the receive this most Holy Sacrament."

The Priest then picks up the two halves of the Host, holding them together in front of him so as to suggest the shape of the *vesica piscis*. He says: "Body of our Lord Jesus Christ, keep me unto Life Eternal," then makes the sign of the cross with the Host and then eats it. While consuming the Host, the Priest genuflects in thoughtful contemplation. Once the Host is fully consumed, the Priest rises and takes up the Holy Chalice of Blood, holds it forth reverently and triumphantly, saying: "Blood of our Lord Jesus Christ, keep me unto Life Eternal." As with the Host, he makes the sign of the cross with the Chalice, and drinks from it. He replaces the Chalice, wipes the rim of the Chalice with the Purificator, then kneels as before in silent meditation. The Priest rises, crosses his arms over his chest in the Good Shepherd position, and says, "There is no part of me that is not part of God." If there are other Bishops or Priests present, they come forth at this time and commune themselves in the same manner. Then the rest of the clergy, and finally the congregants are called

117

forth to receive communion. There are a couple of different ways that this may be carried out, equally acceptable. The Host and Chalice may be given separately, wherein the Chalice rim would be wiped after every drink. Alternatively, the Host may be dipped in the Blood and served together. Likewise, it may be taken in the mouth or in the hand. These are decisions to be made by each celebrant as he or she sees fit for the particular gathering. While serving the communicants, the Priest says, "Body of our Lord Jesus Christ, keep you unto Life Eternal...Blood of our Lord..." etc. or, if the Host is dipped: "Body and Blood of our Lord..." etc. After communicating, the communicant does as the Priest before, assuming the sign of the Good Shepherd and declaring: "There is no part of me that is not part of God." This statement is a reflection of the transformative power of the Eucharist, by which, according to Robert Ambelain in his *Spiritual Alchemy*:

...we absorb an occult and mystic "charge," a philter of immortality which, if we impregnate ourselves with it sufficiently and often enough during the course of our terrestrial life, could transmute us little by little, year by year. For this "charge," assimilated by our organism like all regular nourishment, nevertheless passes from the physiological plane to the psyche, and from the psyche into the nous, *or spirit.*

Once everybody has received Communion, the Priest places any crumbs that may be remaining upon the Paten into the Chalice, and drinks the remaining Blood. A little wine and water is then poured into the Chalice and consumed, followed by pouring water only into the Chalice, which is likewise consumed by the Priest. The Chalice is wiped out with the Purificator, and the Paten and Veil are replaced over the Chalice. This concludes the rite of the Communion proper.

Post Eucharistic Prayer

This prayer is recited by all, who are now united in body, soul, and spirit with Christ and with each other. At the cue of the Priest, all say together:

"May we, who in this Holy Mystery have entered into the all-pervading strength and love of Christ our Indwelling Lord, be guided by the Divine Presence into the fullness of Truth, that we may attain to that mount of vision whereon we may see the boundless light unveiled in the wholeness of its Divine Glory. Amen."

Third Hermetic Discourse called the Concluding Rite

You will note that the order of recitation returns here to a clockwise pattern. That is because, having accomplished our intimate union, there is nothing left to do but to spread this light and blessing unto the world. With this clockwise motion of the spoken parts, one should envision the great peace and harmony that now reigns in the Temple spreading outward, into the community, the country, the planet, and the cosmos. Each should see oneself as a radiant beacon of light and life.

Let us look at each part of the Concluding Rite separately. The Priest begins:

"If thou wilt not equal thyself to God, thou canst not understand God. Increase thyself unto an immeasurable greatness, leaping beyond everybody and transcending all time; become eternity and thou shalt understand God. If thou believe in thyself that nothing is impossible, but accountest thyself immortal, thou canst understand all things; every art, every science, and the manner and custom of every living thing."

So, that's not too much to ask, right? In all seriousness, though, what is described here is precisely the result of the successful attainment of Theosis, or deification. The idea behind theosis is that "God became man, that man might become god." This process, briefly, consists of a stage of purification called *Catharsis* (coming from the same Greek root as *Cathar*); a stage of enlightenment, called *Theoria*; and a final stage of deification called *Theosis*. This doctrine arose from the Eastern Orthodox tradition, but has a great applicability within Gnosticism. For more on this process, please see our "Theosis Through Gnosis." For a description of a similar process, that of *Katharismos*, *Photismos*, and *Henosis,* see Tau Palamas' *Syzygy* and *Inflame Thyself*, both of which works give profound insight and helpful applications of this process. Let us continue our examination of this Discourse with the words of the 1st Deacon:

"Become higher than all height, lower than all depths, comprehend in thyself the qualities of all the Creatures of the Fire, the Water, the Dry and the Moist; and conceive likewise, that thou canst at once be everywhere, in the Sea, in the Earth, in the Air."

This is a pretty standard expression of the Hermetic philosophy, which states that, man being a microcosm, to know Nature and its laws is to know oneself. That is to say that the various processes of human biology and psychology are to be seen mirrored in the processes of Nature at every level, from the lowest to the highest. This statement also suggests that consciousness is not strictly limited to the body; that it can be expanded, potentially infinitely. There are, in fact, multiple layers of meaning here; and through contemplation and meditation, one may attain new levels of understanding, even approaching the Gnosis itself. Let us continue by looking at the 2nd Deacon's part:

"Thou shalt at once understand thyself, not yet begotten, in the womb, young, old, to be dead, the things after death, and all these together; as also times, places, deeds, qualities, quantities; or else thou canst not yet understand God."

We see the general theme continued here. It is the theme of the expansion of consciousness to include not only all parts of Nature, but also every stage of the Natural Cycle. This is exactly what the initiatic tradition helps us to do. The initiatic tradition is the natural and necessary counterpart to the sacramental tradition. The sacraments deal with a divine power that flows through us like channels. Receiving the apostolic succession does not necessarily impart any "powers"; rather it opens pathways through which the Divine Powers may flow. Initiation, on the other hand, while not directly imparting either Gnosis or occult powers, gives one the psychological tools by which one may develop them for him or herself. It is through the initiatic process that one first comes to understand the various stages of life and death in the Lesser Mysteries; and in the Greater Mysteries to develop one's latent abilities and to commune with the Higher Intelligences, and to eventually act as a great force for good on this planet and in the universe. The modern Gnostic movement has the great benefit of being bound to both the sacramental and initiatic traditions.

To close this first "stanza" the Priest and the Deacons say together: "For the light is One and its Mystery is a hiddenness beyond our senses and beyond the vision of our eyes." This statement serves as a bridge between the first and second parts. Since the second section is shorter, let us look at all three parts together:

PRIEST: In all things that are, are the senses, because they cannot be without them.

1st DEACON: But Gnosis differs much from sense; for sense is of the things that surmount it, but Gnosis is the end of sense.

2nd DEACON: Gnosis is the gift of God; for all Gnosis is unbodily, but useth the Mind as an instrument, as the Mind uses the body.

We see here the transition from the lesser to the Greater Mysteries; from the study of Nature and its cycles, to a transrational Gnosis of Divine things. We learn here that the senses are only useful to the extent that we wish to know of the things that act upon those senses; but that there is a higher knowledge that begins where the senses end. The tripartite nature of the human being is also discernible here; for just as the Mind, that is to say the consciousness (which is our psychical faculty) utilizes the brain (our hylic instrument) in order to manifest itself, Gnosis, which is of a pneumatic nature, is expressed through the Mind, or psyche.

The Priest and the Deacons, to transition to the conclusion of this part, say together: "Therefore I believe Thee, and bear witness, and go into the Life and Light." The Priest then says, as a blessing to the people, "The Life and Light of God be with you." To which all respond, "And with thy spirit."

Dismissal

The Dismissal is a very important part of the Mass. It not only concludes the work and sends everybody on their way, but also serves to dismiss all of the unbodily beings who have been in attendance: Archangels, the Angel of the Mass, the Saints and Passed Masters, and any other beings, entities, or elementals that may have found themselves attracted by the mighty spiritual light pulsing like a lighthouse beacon. Likewise, at the final blessing, all of these beings receive a share of that benediction, according to what they are able to receive. This also gives the final instruction for living in the Light and maintaining that intimate communion with Christ. There is really nothing left to comment upon here, so let us read this final Dismissal of the Priest:

"From our sanctuary here, may the Light be spread throughout the world. May Christ the Logos of the Eternal Aeon, show you the Light that you seek, give you His comfort and compassion, and lead you to true Wisdom."

"Solomon in his great wisdom said to his son: Do thou, O my son Roboam, remember, that the fear of the Lord is only the beginning of Wisdom. Keep of preserve those who have not Understanding in the Fear of the Lord, which will give and will preserve unto thee my crown. But learn to triumph thyself over fear by Wisdom, and the Spirits will descend from Heaven to serve thee."

"I, Solomon, thy father, King of Israel and Palmyra, I have sought out and obtained in my lot the Holy Chokhmah, which is the Wisdom of Adonai. And I have become King of the Spirits, as well of Heaven as of Earth, Master of the Dwellers of the Air, and of the Living Souls of the Sea, because I was in possession of the Key of the Hidden Gates of Light."

"There is a peace that passes all understanding; it abides in the hearts of those who live in the eternal now. There is a power that makes all things new; it lives and moves in those who know themselves as one."

"May that peace abide with you; may that power lift you up to the awareness wherein dwells the Christ, so that you may look with your eyes unveiled upon His most Holy Countenance and there see your true self revealed."

"And may the blessing of the Mystery of the Three-in-One, of God the Unknown Father + of Christ the redeeming and ever-coming Logos + and of the Holy Spirit our celestial Mother and Consoler + descend upon you and remain with you always. Amen."

      In closing, the Priest pronounces the traditional dismissal: "Ite, missa est," which means, in essence, "Go, the mass is ended." All respond to this with the words "Deo gratias," or "Thanks be to God." At these words the Mass is concluded and the Recession begins. The clergy recession occurs slightly differently than the initial procession. The Minor Order clergy rise and proceed to the entrance into the antechamber. Without yet entering the Pronaos, they open the door and stand to either side, lined up so as to form an aisle, with their right hand over the heart. Meanwhile, the celebrants of the Mass circumambulate the altar counter-clockwise. The Priest begins by turning to his or her right and walking slowly around the altar in a counter-clockwise motion. When the Priest has completed one full circuit, the 1st Deacon immediately begins a similar movement. When the Priest has returned to the point of origin for the second time, and the 1st Deacon having made one complete circuit, the 2nd Deacon joins in for the final round. After the third complete circuit has been made by the Priest, they continue their recession towards the door to the antechamber. They are followed by any non-celebrating and guest clergy. After passing through the aisle of Minor Order clergy and exiting the Temple into the Pronaos, the Minor Order clergy follow behind, beginning with those furthest from the door, alternating left and right, until the last Porter exits, closing the door behind them. A Porter then goes around to the main entrance of the Temple and opens the door for the congregation to depart.

Conclusion

This short treatment on the Mass cannot possibly do justice to the rich experience of participating in the Mass, or to the varied and multiple teachings to be imparted thereby. But perhaps, at least, we have been able to do slightly more than just scratch the surface. It has been our endeavor to penetrate a little here and there into some of the more obscure recesses of the Liturgical rite.

The Holy Gnostic Liturgy of the Pleromic Light has been found by us, and by many who have reported to us of its efficacy, to be an incredibly powerful Theurgical rite. Effecting the Eucharistic transubstantiation is one thing. But the present Liturgy goes much further. In our discussion above on the Third Hermetic Discourse, we mentioned the importance of wedding the sacramental to the initiatic. This Liturgy does just that. Through its form, language, and the various apostolic and initiatic currents flowing through the episcopacy of the ACP, the Liturgy of the Pleromic Light, when celebrated by one suitably empowered, brings together the powerful energies and essences of Apostolic Gnosticism, Martinism, and occult Freemasonry, which, collectively, make up the true Rose+Croix.

The Light of the Rose+Croix was the original guiding impetus behind the initial stages of development of this Liturgy nearly twenty years ago, and it has remained the Vital Force of its fruition and execution. It is truly hoped that this brief treatise will lead you not only to a better understanding of the Liturgy of the Pleromic Light, but to a deeper and richer experience of its celebration. May the Light of Gnosis and the blessings of the Three-in-One be spread to all who read these words. So mote it be.

Works Cited or Mentioned

Aland, Kurt, Matthew Black, Carlo M. Martini, Bruce
    M. Metzger, and Alan Wikgren, eds. *Greek New
    Testament*, Fourth Corrected Edition. United Bible
    Societies, 1993.

Ambelain, Robert. *Abbé Julio: His Life, His Work, His
    Doctrine*. Hainesville, IL: Triad Press, LLC, 2016.
    — *Spiritual Alchemy: The Inner Path*. 1961. Trans.
    Piers Vaughan, 2005.

Anson, Peter. *Bishops at Large*. Berkeley: Apocryphile
    Press, 2006.

Consultation on Common Texts. *Revised Common
    Lectionary*. Minneapolis: Augsburg Fortress Pub.,
    1992.

Julio, Abbé. *Grand Marvelous Secrets*. Hainesville, IL:
    Triad Press, LLC, 2016.
    — *Liturgical Prayers*. Hainesville, IL: Triad Press,
    LLC, 2016.
    — *Secret Book of Grand Exorcisms and Benedictions*.
    Hainesville, IL: Triad Press, LLC, 2016

Leadbeater, Charles. *Science of the Sacraments*. Adyar:
    Theosophical Publishing House, 1929.

Liturgies of the Ecclessia Gnostica Catholica Hermetica.
    Zion, IL: Triad Press, LLC, 2005.

Mathers, S.L. MacGregor. *The Key of Solomon the   King*.
    London: G. Redway, 1889. (Dover fac. 2009.)

Mead, G.R.S., trans. *Pistis Sophia*. Mineola, NY: Dover
    Publications, Inc., 2005.

Nestle, Eberhard and Erwin, Barbara and Kurt Aland,
    Johannes Karavidopoulos, Carlo M. Martini, and
    Bruce M. Metzger, eds. *Novum Testamentum, Graece
    et Latine*, Editio XXVII. Stuttgart: Deutsche
    Bibelgesellschaft, 1994.

Palamas, Tau. *Spirit Builders: A Free Illuminist Approach to
    the Antient and Primitive Rite of Memphis+Misraim*.

Cobb, CA: Transmutation Publishing, 2015.

— *Syzygy: Reflections on the Monastery of the Seven Rays*, Annotated Second Edition. Cobb, CA: Transmutation Publishing, 2015.

— *Inflame Thyself.* Cobb, CA: Transmutation Publishing, unp. mss.

Papus (Dr. Gérard Encausse). "Esotercism of the Pater Noster." http://pleromachurch.org.

— "Meditations on the 'Pater.'" http://pleromachurch.org.

Pasqually, Martinès de. *Treatise on the Reintegration of Beings*. Hainesville, IL: Triad Press, LLC, 2016.

Phosphoros, Tau. *Apostolic Church of the Pleroma Clergy Handbook*. Hainesville, IL: Triad Press, LLC, 2014.

— "Alchemy of the Eucharist."

— "The Devil's Passion."

— "A Gnostic Exposition of the Three Alchemical Essentials."

— "On the Eucharist."

Phosphoros, Tau. *Apostolic Church of the Pleroma Lectionary for Mass*. Hainesville, IL: Triad Press, LLC, 2014.

Phosphoros, Tau. "Brief Analysis of the ACP Seal. http://pleromachurch.org, 2013.

— "Successio Apostolica." http://pleromachurch.org, 2012.

— "The Tetragrammaton in the Three Worlds." http://pleromachurch.org, 2015.

— "Theosis Through Gnosis." http://pleromachurch.org, 2015.

Plummer, John. *The Many Paths of the Independent Sacramental Movement*. Berkeley: Apocryphile Press, 2005.

Wagner, Wynn. *The Complete Liturgy for Independent, Mystical, and Liberal Catholics*. Dallas: Mystic Way Books, 2010.

www.ingramcontent.com/pod-product-compliance
Lightning Source LLC
Chambersburg PA
CBHW022012090426
42741CB00007B/995